Prophet of a New Hindu Age

Prophet of a New Hindu Age

The Life and Times of Acharya Pranavananda

NINIAN SMART
and
SWAMI PURNANANDA

London
GEORGE ALLEN & UNWIN
Boston   Sydney

George Allen & Unwin (Publishers) Ltd,
40 Museum Street, London WC1A 1LU, UK

George Allen & Unwin (Publishers) Ltd,
Park Lane, Hemel Hempstead, Herts HP2 4TE, UK

Allen & Unwin Inc.,
Fifty Cross Street, Winchester, Mass 01890, USA

George Allen & Unwin Australia Pty Ltd,
8 Napier Street, North Sydney, NSW 2060, Australia

George Allen & Unwin with the Port Nicholson Press
PO Box 11–838 Wellington, New Zealand

First published in 1985

ISBN 0 04 922032 2 cased
0 04 922033 0

Set in 11 on 13 point Imprint by Phoenix Photosetting Ltd, Chatham
and printed in Great Britain by Mackays of Chatham Ltd

CONTENTS

CONTENTS

INTRODUCTION

This book is an account of the life of the remarkable Bengali spiritual and practical leader, Swami Pranavananda, who lived in the first half of the twentieth century. He was only 44 when he died but he left his imprint on India in various ways. He was born in what is now Bangladesh and strove to realise, in the order he founded (his Sangha), an organisation which would bring new energy, life and pride to the Hindu masses of India. As will be seen from the narrative, his work and ideals went well beyond this. He was one of the figures whom we ought to take seriously in estimating the power and value of the modern Hindu renaissance, stretching from Ram Mohan Roy to contemporary times when a variety of new religious leaders have made their impact upon both the Indian and the Western scene. His type of spirituality is very different in certain ways from that of other *gurus* and saints whose lives have come to the attention of the English-reading public. In some ways he stands most authentically for ancient Hindu values which can easily be overlooked by modern commentators, scholars and interpreters of religion. Perhaps he is the most conspicuous case of the practice of *tapasya* in modern times. It will be seen from this book how remarkable his self-discipline and self-training were. Quite apart from this, his achievements were such that his life deserves to be better known than it is to the wider world.

Some years ago I was approached by Swami Purnananda (a direct and close disciple of the Acharya for sixteen years) of the London Branch of the Bharat Sevashram Sangha with a view to our working together to bring out a book about Swami Pranavananda. The book has taken its present shape in the following way. Swami Purnananda gave me a copy of a manuscript he had been working on outlining the life and teachings of the Acharya (as our subject was also called). I took this material and used it as a general basis for writing an account. I also made use of some other material, including the biography (rather brief but quite useful) by Swami Vedananda. I have written the book in a way which is intended to bring out the Hindu background and to some extent the political background of the Acharya's activities. I have concentrated mainly on giving a sense of the actual fabric of the Hinduism in which the Acharya was himself so important a strand. In this way the book may have a more general interest, for it is itself an introduction to many of the main features of the Hindu way of life. As Hinduism serves, so to speak, as a window on the Acharya so this life of the Acharya may serve as a window on Hinduism. Many readers may find that their views of the Hindu tradition alter somewhat when seen from this particular angle.

It is to be hoped that this account of the Acharya may stimulate others to go further. But the necessities of human existence dictate that most of those who worked with the Acharya up to his death in 1941 have either passed from the scene or may not have too long to live, and so it was important to record something of his life a little more fully than has been done hitherto while still there remains an immediate link with him. There is further research to be done, too, in the newspapers and archives of the period. Substantially this biography is a supplemented version of the memoirs put together by Swami Purnananda.

It should be borne in mind that the book aims to be faithful to two principles. On the one hand it is important as far as possible to present the historical facts about the Acharya's life and activities; but at the same time it is vital for us to glimpse something of his person as seen through the eyes of those who had faith in him and followed him in his arduous calling. I have tried in this latter respect to be what is sometimes called 'phenomenological'; or – to put it more simply – to see the Acharya through the eyes of those for whom he was a divinely-inspired leader. On the whole I have not otherwise given an evaluation of him, save that in the last chapter there are reflections upon his significance for modern India and in the wider perspective of religion. I have tried to let the meaning of the extraordinary events of his life shine through as they would be perceived not just by the English-speaking, Western reader but also by the monks and masses for whom he was a heroic figure. Never judge a person until you have walked a mile in his moccasins, as the proverb says. So I have, I hope, provided an empathetic account both of his life and of the Hindu environment in which he lived.

Apart from the way in which the Acharya can be understood as a powerful figure in the Hindu tradition, we can also reflect on what he means for the wider world. First, if his dynamism has helped to create a new consciousness within Hinduism which can lead to a restoration of Hindu values and a flourishing of genuine religion in the sub-continent, this is something of vital moment to global civilisation, in which Hindu values must surely play a major role. Second, his accent on austerity presents an ideal from which many outside India can learn. It represents an authentic ancient value which has been underestimated in modern times, so the Acharya's life in this way is an example for human beings to contemplate.

There is much that is mysterious in the workings of the religious world. Strange energies pulse through it. The achievements of the Acharya (or of God working through him) were startling, and it is therefore with a sense both of fascination and gratitude that I have been working on this project with Swami Purnananda, himself a fine testimony to the power of inspiration in the Sangha which he represents.

Ninian Smart
Lancaster
England

November 25, 1984

1
THE CHILDHOOD
OF A YOGI

Around the birth of a saint there cluster legends. Parents recall significant dreams. Neighbours remember strange signs. Later biographers seek for meaning in the date. All this is true of Swami Pranavananda, whose story and place in Indian spirituality and political history this book unfolds. He was born in 1896, in a water-girt village in what is now Bangladesh but which was then part of that greater India over which the British presided. It was at the beginning of the greatest and most fruitful period of Indian modernity: the period which saw the ultimate success of the nationalist movement, during just over half a century of powerful debate, turmoil, war and struggle. 1896 was a year of both suffering and new hope.

It was in the middle of a dreadful period of famines and plagues, especially in Bengal. But it was also the year when, on the other side of India, in Maharashtra, the Shivaji festival was founded by a militant nationalist, Lokamanya Tilak. Shivaji had been the founder of the Mahratta empire which had broken away from Mughal rule in the seventeenth century, and so had prepared the example of a Hindu Raj to set against both the Muslims and later the British. Tilak, in founding a new militancy, trod a path which ultimately the majority of the Congress Party, under the leadership of Nehru and Gandhi, was not going to take. A more moderate and non-violent nationalism was to prove more adequate to the task of prising away Britain's grip. But Tilak's strong patriotism was important in representing a promise of revolt which the British could never ignore.

1

Only three years before 1896, a highly significant event had occurred in the unimaginably distant city of Chicago. There the dynamic Bengali religious teacher Vivekananda, disciple of the saintly Ramakrishna, had made a great impact on the so-called Parliament of Religions held in connection with a World Fair. Vivekananda's message of the universality of Hinduism, as a faith embracing many different paths to the Divine, had given quite a new perspective on the Indian tradition – a perspective new, that is, to Westerners, who had hitherto mainly encountered missionary reports of strange images and dark cults. Vivekananda's message was to become the heart of a modern Hindu ideology which helped at the same time to express a pluralistic nationalism. Both the militancy of Tilak and the universalism of Vivekananda were to remain important ingredients in the Indian national struggle, and were important features of the background to the future Swami Pranavananda's life and thought.

1893 was also the year that Gandhi had gone to South Africa where, over the next twenty-one years, he was to forge new weapons with which to return to a now restless India near the start of the First World War. It was, then, at a propitious time that young Binode was born in Bajitpur, about two hundred miles east of Calcutta.

He was born into a traditional Hindu setting. Like many other such villages in India, Bajitpur was in effect a cluster of settlements. But unlike those in most parts of the great sub-continent it was a very watery place. A branch of the river Kumar twisted through the area, forming streams and ponds between which were placed different settlements accommodating various castes and groups – the Brahmins whose purity and high status made them the chief repository of ancient Vedic rituals and teachings, the intermediate *Kayasthas*, the lowly *Sudras*, the Muslims and the untouchables. The streams and ponds could cater for the drinking, washing and ritual requirements of the different groups. Here was a model, in some ways, of the wider pluralism which much of modern Indian thinking has tried to express: different castes and religions living together in a fashion, close but separated. And everywhere water – sometimes inundating the whole area, washing into the yards, brimming up towards the houses and giving the village the aspect of a fleet of boats, surrounding the fruit-trees, washing away dirt and bathing away the causes of sickness, renewing the soil and enriching the next season's harvest, filling the broad fields that stretched round Bajitpur, tearing away the creepers and flowers that in drier seasons embellished the paths and yards beside the huddled houses and beneath the varied trees.

In Binode's day there were, too, the four temples and other shrines which helped to focus the religious life of the area. There was a Sanskrit school with its traditional pundit, and later there was to rise the English-language high school, the major key to moving onwards in the new hierarchy of learning and employment grafted on to India by the British. But although here was a symbol of that wider world into which India was moving willy-nilly, the rhythms of the village were primordial. They were times without time.

Life in the village was not a matter of diaries and printed calendars but of the change of seasons, the phases of the moon, the rising of the sun and its setting. The year revolved in the minds of men and women who anticipated the festivals and traditional routines and duties. Tradition produces a matrix out of which the stuff of life is daily fashioned. Despite the floods, storms and plagues that beset Bengali life, the people had security in the repeated structures of time which bind lives together. For each festival and each routine, whether of sowing or harvesting or housecleaning, reminded a person of his brothers and sisters in the fabric of village life with whom he shared joys and tribulations. Life was warm, humid, patterned by sacred events, glimmering with the traces of the glorious past, and haunted by the gods who were the outer messengers of the one Divine Being.

The interpreters of these messengers were, as often as not, the old folk. Grandparents in such a milieu delighted in telling the ancient epic stories of the *Rāmāyaṇa* and the *Mahābhārata* – those immense mixtures of adventure and

3

high derring-do on the one hand and spiritual and ethical teachings on the other. For village India it was as if John Buchan, Fenimore Cooper, Tolkien and the Pentateuch were blended together, so that the young absorbed the values of the Hindu world as they sat around the cots of the old men late into the night. Thus they were kept in touch with the timeless values of seers who conveyed to the human race the sacred utterances of the Vedas and the spellbinding teachings of the Song of the Lord. They could listen to the village boatman cry at dusk 'Hari Lord, the day has gone, evening has come, guide me across the stream of life'. As they were prepared themselves to cross that river, the children, wide-eyed and eager, would call on their elders to repeat the sacred tales which wound long, even endlessly, through the adventures of gods, humans and demons in Ayodhya and Lanka and the ancient battlefields of Bharata, of old India. In this way the village was linked dimly but firmly to a sense of a huge, unitary past: and now that past was being mobilised anew as a consciousness of Indian identity was being stimulated by alien rule and alien educational values. But this new national sense was only a ripple as yet on the surface of village life in Bajitpur.

The rhythms of the Hindu festivals are complex, and it was within this dense pattern of living that the young Binode came to consciousness. He was to see the astrologers come to the house during the first week of *Baisakh*, in the middle of April, at the start of the Hindu year. They would exhibit their learning and their knowledge of the heavenly bodies whose subtle influences helped to shape human destinies. Astrology was, and is in most of India still, respected as a vital science by which social life could and should be regulated. One should not run contrary to the stars; and days for weddings, all kinds of larger endeavours in daily life, plans for leaving home to go to market or to college – all such were undertaken in the light of the reasoning and observations of the professional exponents of *jyotish*, star-science. The boy would listen to their thoughts about the coming year and whether its seasons boded good or ill. It was a subtle affair, for blended with the heavenly influences were the

4

natural powers of things, the karma of living beings, the activities of gods, the will of the Creator. All these affected human life and all should be studied seriously by those who wished to understand why things happen as they do.

In July and August came the monsoon, when the village would take on its aspect as a fleet. It was time, too, to honour snakes, those obscure and vibrant repositories of sacred power, beautiful in their sheeny skins and kindly in action if only humans treated them with respect; time to offer milk for their delectation, and honour their divine role in the wider dispensation of the gods as symbols of time, promisers of fertility, reminders of creation. Also in August came the date of the Lord Krishna's birth. Not all those in the village would directly participate, for not all were followers of Vishnu and his charming, heroic, dashing, sacred avatar, Krishna. But who in the village could fail to be affected by this Christmas of the Hindu year? Binode, like other children, could take joy in the example of the by no means solemn childhood and youth of blue Krishna, chubby in face, with cascades of black curls running round and down his lovely head.

October was the time of Durga, a most powerful deity in Bengal and beyond, but especially in Bengal. It was a time for getting new clothes and parading through the village – the Easter, as it were, of the Hindu world. The beautiful and fiercely impressive figure of Durga, reflecting the powers of divine creation and destruction, was the focus of sacrifice. The brahmins presided, and the sacrificial specialist would slaughter the goats before the image. The wild and insistent drums, the chants, the glory of the feast, would create an intense excitement that even the Muslims and the Harijans (although excluded from the rituals) would sense and enjoy. And so the year moved on. There was the festival to Lakshmi, sweet consort of Vishnu; the time of lights; the special festival for those who work in iron (bringing joy and power to the blacksmiths' quarter in the rambling village); the time for honouring the forefathers, when heads of families did reverence to the ancestors (themselves part of the wider, invisible society in which the living are embedded); the

5

sibling festival when sisters honoured brothers with a dot of sandal paste on the forehead, thus reinforcing the bonds of the family. There was the feast of Sarasvati, goddess of learning, when education itself was worshipped, the high school was a riot of colour and great processions took out the clay-built statue of the goddess and wound their way through the village until the impermanent image was drowned joyfully in the river (for life moves on, and the images were as impermanent and kaleidoscopic as anything else in this glory-filled universe). Finally the year drew to a close in March and April. During this time there was the Shiva festival, when the God was taken in procession by the untouchables and high caste Hindus celebrated one of the great orthodox representations of Deity, the great Yogi Shiva, auspicious one, frighteningly powerful creator and destroyer, personifying the immense cosmic cycles of emergence and fiery collapse. The eve of the New Year was at hand – a joyful time of village fairs, of sweets for the children and money for little toys, a time when fathers bought supplies of spices for the coming year and wives prepared delicacies for the visitors on this last day – priests who came to celebrate end-of-year ceremonials in each house and themselves received food and offerings, while those who wished to considered what vows to make for the coming year. The rich gained merit by organising public meals. The temple bells and drums sounded. The whole day and night were occupied with the repetition of God's name; and the fairs abounded with sweets, little toys and feats of magic and music.

All this of course was superimposed on grimmer realities. The labour of the paddies and rice fields could be seriously disturbed by flooding, crops destroyed, children deprived. There were, then as now, large numbers of poor people; disease sometimes struck the mosquito-infested villages; malaria and amoebic dysentery were endemic. But despite these troubles and sufferings, a way of life had given shape, meaning and joy to the annual cycle. It provided for the Hindu a background of divinity, as it still does. The continuous singing of religious songs can be heard from a temple, paid for by the local rich: there is daily feeding of the poor; bells clang before the temple deities; and meanwhile in every Hindu household, regular offerings are made and rituals performed. It is a highly structured life, although belied sometimes by the appearance of chaotic bustle in the village and its satellites. Even in 1896 the number of people gave a semblance of chaos and today the pressures of population are even greater.

This was the village background – not without its idyllic side, even if it were laced with divisions, sufferings and anxieties – of the first years of Binode, later to be known as Acharya Pranavananda. Clearly there was much there, to any young person so predisposed, which would stimulate the religious sense. He was born on 29 January, during the holy month of *Magha*, towards dusk, when Hindus offer prayers both at the temple and in the home. For his later followers the time was auspicious; as one sun sank so another sun was rising. The full moon of *Magha*, as of other months, was a sacred turning point in the calendar, and it also coincided with the beginning of the present epoch in Hindu cosmic history, the *Kali Yuga*, which had begun five thousand years before.

The *Kali Yuga* is not a fortunate time to be alive, even if it contains great and holy figures who can arrest human decline by recalling humanity to the holy *dharma* or teaching. In previous epochs of the present aeon, life was more blessed and spacious. This is a common theme of Indian thought (and is shared with some other cultures). Not for them the easy assumption of human progress; rather a sense that life and virtue are decaying, sliding downwards. Thus Binode was born into a society which was on the brink of a contradictory, dualised world-view. The new national struggle promised a fresh beginning, a liberation, a revitalised India of the future. It contained the message of freedom and implied the modernist, evolutionary eschatology of progress. But older thought was more pessimistic, rooted in concepts of falling away from more golden ages. In the Kali Yuga

7

humanity is afflicted by diseases, both physical and spiritual. It is rare for men to live beyond a hundred years. Religion is in decline, and various forms of viciousness are on the increase. Homosexuality is rife, as is heterosexual promiscuity. The *dharma*, in other words, is no longer preserved and this, in itself, affects the health of society. Still, there are those who struggle against this downward flowing stream: they swim higher. They are saints and human beings of great virtue. And their births are typically attended by all kinds of signs.

Binode's parents were called Bishnu Charan Das and Sumati Devi. They were a pious couple belonging to the Kayastha caste which is variously classified in different places and regions. Its members range from landowners and bureaucrats to merchants and lawyers. As a minor land-owner, Bishnu was part of the Bengali system of those days. He was subagent of the local major landlord or *zamindar* and had the task of collecting rents on his behalf. These larger landlords had of course an interest in squeezing the peasants, and agents could either become harsh enforcers of an increasingly oppressive system or act as buffers against their superiors. Bishnu, being a pious person who took virtue and mercy seriously, adopted the latter course. This brought him into conflict with Rajkumar Majumdar, the local landlord, and his managers, who tried to pressurise him with accusations and legal processes. A civil suit against him was to drag on for some twenty years – not uncommon in India then or even now – although an attempt to implicate Bishnu Das in the murder of two Bajitpur villagers was dismissed by the magistrate.

After the birth of Binode, Bishnu's luck in regard to the law began to pick up, and he attributed his success as somehow due to the boy and his special relationship with God. As is not unusual in such cases his parents later looked back on certain dreams they had had before his birth as highly significant. They both had intimations that their future child was to be a manifestation of Lord Shiva. Sumati had a dream vision of Shiva turning into a baby whose exquisite aura filled the whole room. It was of course a common belief among such pious Hindus as Bishnu and Sumati that God adopts a human form and that both Shiva and Vishnu were liable to appear as humans from time to time in order to restore the holy teaching and the love of virtue in periods of chaos and degeneration like the present epoch.

Early events in the boy's life were, they thought, confirmations of his exceptional nature. For one thing he seemed remarkably serene, not given to crying or making demands. The rumours that perhaps he was a manifestation of Shiva had spread and peasant families sometimes came to the house hoping for a power-enhancing glimpse of the divine child. His parents, impressed by his manner and intimations of his higher destiny, let him do much as he pleased and were no doubt surprised when he got them to give him an outhouse to use, and transformed it into a place of study and meditation. Even as a young boy, before his initiation into the life of the pious, upper-class Hindu, he was practising being a holy ascetic, preparing himself for his future career. Although his family ate fish and meat he remained vegetarian and kindly attempts to make him at least eat fish, for otherwise he might become sickly, resulted in his vomiting it up. He was it seemed a natural vegetarian. Indeed, he was very strict, for he even refused milk and ghee; and despite the remonstrations of the family priest, one Mahendra Chakravarty, he kept to this regime. His physique was strong and healthy. Apart from questions of the impurity which is brought upon one by eating flesh, Hindus often think of food in terms of the various forms of energy it generates. For the future Acharya there was always an abundance of energy, so he thought, so that taking these animal substances would give him a dangerous excess. The boy spent many hours in his outhouse trying out forms of traditional austerity or *tapas*. India and the Bengali milieu provided him with a great variety of heroes and role-models. What might seem to the modern Westerner peculiar and even rather precious (for children's piety can indeed be sickly), could have been natural enough for Binode; his parents' dreams and the rumours of peasants

9

gave substance to the thought that here was a child destined for great things in the life of the spirit.

He was supposed, moreover, to have had a spiritual experience of great power when he was very young. The story was told by him many years later, when he was already in his 20s, but there is no reason to doubt the authenticity of the account. He referred to the experience in conversation with Swami Purnananda, for instance, in October 1924, when he said: 'My first God-realisation came to me at the age of 6'. Some think that this is a very early age for such an event. But already, as we have noted, the child was orienting himself towards the spiritual. Indeed if children can be precocious in music like Mozart or in philosophy like Shankara, why not in the numinous like Binode? The story is as follows.

One day he had climbed on to the roof of the family home, which was flat like that of most well-built Indian dwellings. Looking down, he saw his mother worshipping the Tulsi plant. This is a form of basil, and sacred to Vishnu. The legend is that there once was a beautiful and saintly woman, who in grief at her husband's death threw herself on to his funeral pyre. Vishnu did not wish her beauty to have been in vain and transformed her body into the Gandaki river in Nepal, also sacred to Vishnu, and an excellent place for finding those black ammonite stones with strange markings – the *śālagrāma* – without which no *Vaiṣṇava* house is complete. Vishnu changed her hair into the sacred basil, the *Tulsi*. This plant Binode's mother was now worshipping, smearing the special brick-girt spot where it grew, circumambulating it in the auspicious clockwise direction, and bowing low before it. For the inquisitive child it was a puzzlement. Why should his mother worship what was only a plant, a condiment? Was it right? Did the plant really have any power? He thought not, so from the roof he spat on to the plant. And this was when he was astonished.

For instantly the god of the plant appeared to him in luminous, human form and reproached him. 'Binode, I am Narayana; I live in the *Tulsi* plant.' Binode forthwith fell into a trance.

It is interesting that the vision was of Vishnu (describing himself here as Narayana, a version of the god most familiar to us in sculpture as reclining on the cosmic snake Shesha). Binode's family were primarily followers of Shiva. But Binode later was to be in the forefront of the movement to synthesise the two great branches of Hinduism, and to see both Shiva and Vishnu as alternate representations of the one Reality.

There is a factor in the Hindu tradition which must be understood in order to grasp something of the spiritual essence of pluralism. It is a factor somewhat alien to Western (Christian, Jewish or Muslim) attitudes. In these Western religions one is classified as either believing in the one God, or else believing in many gods, which is both polytheism and idolatry. We shall return to the question of so-called idolatry a little later; but as for polytheism, the fact is that at first sight Hinduism, for the Westerner, is pure polytheism. A famous account of Hindu myth and ritual, by Alain Danielou, is entitled *Hindu Polytheism*. Certainly there are myths of many gods. But the Hindu case is not one of either-or. It is a case of believing in both the one and the many. It is difficult for us with our traditional Western categories to grasp this. It is as if the One Divine Being becomes refracted into the many figures of divine beings which animate the rich store-house of Hindu myth. The properties of God hive off to become individual divinities. God's power becomes his female consort (Shiva becomes Kali or Durga); his playful-ness becomes incarnated in the young Krishna; his learning becomes Sarasvati and so on. The many gods are really so many fragments or refractions of the One. So both Vishnu and Shiva, superficially considered to be rival deities, are alternative representations of the One. This attitude is what may be described as 'refracted theism'. It is neither the austere monotheism of the Western faiths nor the chaotic polytheism of the Greeks. So for the child Binode, the appearance of Narayana-Vishnu was part of that whole, mysteriously refracted, spiritual scene.

He seemed to accept the visitation as natural. If he fell into a kind of trance, it was shortlived. He was to exhibit in later life a dynamic desire to transform the world, not to withdraw from it. But from a religious perspective, why should God reveal himself through a mere plant? Even the monotheisms of the Western world are not without a similar conception – God spoke to Moses through a burning bush, a mere bush in the dry desert. The lesson is, from a Hindu point of view, that the One manifests itself all through nature, in varied forms, so that we may, as Blake says:

> 'See a world in a grain of sand
> And a heaven in a wild flower;
> Hold infinity in the palm of your hand
> And eternity in an hour.'

As a Gnostic saying of Jesus has it: 'Raise the stone and there you will find me; cleave the wood and there I am.' This kind of Gnostic idea is deeply woven into the fabric of Hindu belief. Narayana's appearance to the young Binode was a startling example of the divine presence becoming very explicit. It also reflected a sense, within the boy's conscience, that his spitting on the plant was a moral affront. The incident helped to deepen his reverence for the world about him.

All this is relevant to his later spirituality and helps to cast light on another common aspect of the Hindu tradition. Whether or not Hindus belong to the Non-Dualist (Advaitin) tradition, the idea that God appears in non-manifest and manifest form runs deep in much Hindu thinking. Later Binode was to take the religious name Prana-vananda. This has two parts: Ananda, meaning 'bliss' or 'joy' and Pranava, meaning 'utterance' and referring more particularly to that mysterious, power-laden syllable Om, which is the audible essence of the ineffable Brahman, the holy Power, the One. It stands for and sums up the formless Ultimate (*nirgunaṁ Brahman*) which lies behind the personal Lord of Creation (the *sagunaṁ Brahman*). The Acharya, like many another saint and yogi of the Hindu tradition, meditated on the formless Ultimate and saw it as indeed the supreme which lies beyond all the qualifications which humans place upon their God. But it is easy to get lost in that ineffable Ultimate, to be absorbed in the oceanlike bliss, of the One. It is equally vital to remember that the One is active through the cosmos and that this active, powerful and loving Deity takes personal, often human, form. So the child's apprehension of the God Vishnu was a counterpart to his early ambition to go the other way, into formless meditation and asceticism. In this simple but striking episode of his vision of the God of the *Tulsi* plant there are packed many of the major themes of modern, resurgent Hinduism: its refracted theism and generous pluralism; the personal nature of the One; the necessity to complement the quietism of absorption by the more formed discipleship of a personal Divinity. Binode as a child may not yet have been aware of his calling to revitalise the symbolic worship of the Hindus; but his experience of Narayana and the *Tulsi* plant was surely relevant to it.

Another incident, a year or two later, is also significant. A neighbour, Hara Bilas Kaviraj, was celebrating the worship of Durga with lavish grandeur and the boy Binode, then 7 or 8 years old, could hear the noise of the feast going on. Durga, the 'far one' is identified with the black Kali, dread consort of Shiva. Both are represented as bloody and fierce, and Durga is a great slayer of demons and other frightening mythic beings. As female both goddesses mingle creative and destructive powers. When the celebrations were finished Binode slipped into the temple, disturbed by the thought that maybe idol worship was wrong. The question had come to him, 'Is it true and does it make sense?' In the temple he sat down in a prayerful attitude without bowing to the Goddess, waiting to see if there were any divine power in the image. After a few minutes the sight of the idol gave place to a vision of the Goddess Durga in all her dazzling radiance. In joy and elation he prostrated himself at her feet.

Binode's question about idolatry was a live issue in the India of his day, not only because the truly religious person is always both drawn to and half-sceptical of the outer symbols of his faith but also because Christian evangelists for more than a century had been highly critical of what they saw as idolatry in Hinduism. The ordinary worshippers' treatment of images, the elaborate ceremonials of waking, bathing, feeding and serving the gods in their idol form, the mass of myths surrounding such particular representations of deity, the giving of sacrifices, particularly the sacrifice of goats to Kali-Durga in Bengal – these phenomena were alien to the missionaries and seemed just like the practices the prophets of the Old Testament had so often denounced as Canaanite or heathen. It smacked of that idolatry which Christian martyrs had renounced in the Roman Empire of their day, at the cost of their lives. So Hindus were and still are in some degree sensitive about the significance of such outer imagery.

Gandhi said that it is human to worship idols. What he had in mind was that every God we worship in fact is represented to us by some mental image or form of words, and these are so to speak projections of our minds. We have to represent to ourselves anything upon which we have set our heart. It does not make an essential difference whether we draw the picture inside our consciousness or put it concretely before us in the shape of a statue or a painting. Even those religions such as Islam and Calvinism, which tend to reject statues and ikons, make use of verbal imagery. It may be that actual stone images encourage certain forms of superstitious manipulations of religion. But in principle, from a Hindu point of view, there is no essential difference between a mental and a stone image. In Hindu philosophy, incidentally, mental images themselves are considered to be formed out of a very subtle kind of matter.

Such more speculative thoughts on the matter were no doubt far from Binode's childish mind. But he showed a combination of sceptical enquiry and religiosity in trying to put the theory of idols to the test.

In line with this early experience was the adult Binode's answer to a Brahmo (a follower of Brahmo Samaj) during a religious rally when as the Acharya, he was attended by thousands of devotees. Kali Nath Roy, a Brahmin preacher following the line of the Brahmo tradition – which was a reforming body of the Hindu renaissance, highly critical of many aspects of traditional, popular Hinduism – came to the Acharya to ask why he should tolerate the cult of idols. Is not God one, absolute, ineffable, unimaginable?

'Idolatry,' said Kali Nath Roy, 'is a great scar on Hinduism; it is as foolish as anything.' Acharya Pranavananda remained silent, and it was as if he projected his own thinking into the Brahmo's mind, for the latter went on: 'But Acharya Shankara, who was the greatest exponent of Monism and a man of divine realisation, himself admitted idolatry and composed and sang hymns in praise of gods and goddesses: he had been preaching in the same breath the personal and the impersonal aspects of God.'

The Acharya took up the thread of the discourse and said: 'Yes, this is exactly the truth. Both the aspects of God are equally true; He is at once the formless and with form. He is omnipotent; nothing is impossible with Him. Why should we limit Him within His formless attribute?'

Maybe Binode's vision of Durga was linked in his mind with a strange incident. He had taken a strong aversion to an old woman servant in the household. Sumati Devi, his mother, had noticed this and kept the servant away from the child. But one day when Binode was alone in the yard, the maidservant picked him up. He screamed and immediately began to develop a rash all over his body. His mother called the doctor, but alarmingly the rash continued. In desperation she took Binode to a shrine in the forest where the faithful sometimes sought cures. It was a spot sacred to Bana Durga, separated by a brook from a cemetery where Binode later was to achieve his highest illumination, for as a young man he used to go there to meditate (following a precept found from ancient times in the Hindu, Buddhist and other Indian traditions, that one should practise contemplation in the presence of death). There was also a Muslim shrine there. People from the surrounding area were in the habit of visiting the sacred place. It was here that Sumati Devi

15

brought the young Binode and placed him at the feet of an image of Durga. Almost immediately his rash was cured.

This area later became the centre from which Pranavananda's movement radiated and was the site of his first *ashram*.

It was no doubt some time after the experience of Durga that Binode had the habit of fishing up from the family pond nearby a lump of mud which he would ask his sister, Hemangini to fashion into a little statue of Shiva. He would worship Shiva through the image then dissolve it in the water again.

We have mentioned that he had a small meditation room made from a converted outhouse. He would spend long hours there, sometimes late into the night, training himself as far as possible to do without sleep. Rumour had it that the family had peeped once through the bamboo side of his hut and seen him in a state of levitation. He was angry once that his sister had looked through a chink in the bamboo and told his mother to tell her off. What it was she saw that was special was never revealed.

Unfortunately his childhood was marred by the bullying he experienced from his older brother, Jitendra Das. He would try to slink away when his brother was in the house. The latter would shout at him to do various jobs for him, and if he refused would beat him mercilessly. Binode would often have to help his brother during his night fishing expeditions, rowing the boat, or holding the fish basket. Once during the rainy season they were fishing in a nearby flooded field and Binode was holding the oar while Jitendra was using a net to catch fish. At one point he got a big fellow which he dumped into the bottom of the boat where it thrashed about with great vigour, trying to escape. Jitendra shouted to the boy to hit the fish with the oar. But Binode just stood there watching vacantly as the fish jumped around.

Jitendra shouted: 'You ass, don't you hear? Hit it, hit it.'

But it was as if Binode was paralysed. He felt he could not hit the humble creature. How could he? Yet he had to obey his rather frightening brother; so he raised the oar ready to strike at the fish but, again, could not bring it down. His brother, enraged, came and grabbed the oar, ready to do the killing himself. But the fish heaved itself higher and managed to jump out of the boat.

'Jackass,' Jitendra shouted, 'through your stupidity alone has this fish run away. I'll break your head now instead with this same oar.' Jitendra raged on, and was still shouting about it when he reached home.

Such bullying may have been a primary reason why the child decided to build himself up physically. He was later to say:

'From my childhood I began to exercise this body, thinking that this would give me the strength of an athlete. There also grew in me a sense of prestige: how could I allow anyone in the area to surpass me in strength? And so I exercised this body, eating only water-soaked rice and drinking only boiled rice water. At first no-one could believe me, but later on they had to change their opinion.'

Like many other Indians he was fascinated by the idea of a special diet. His austere one, it seemed to him, was effective. As stories about his unusual physical strength grew, people would come from far and wide to try to squeeze his palm in theirs with a handshake. Sometimes he found them hard to overcome but he generally won these handgrip contests and reflected that their richer diets did his opponents no good.

Until he was 10 or older he usually wore no clothes at all like a traditional holy man; later he typically wore only a loincloth. Since poor men went about like this, what need had he of jacket and *dhoti*? In this as in other matters, Binode seems to have been gripped with a strong sense of personal autonomy, dignity and independence.

Although unusual and eccentric in these ways, Binode apparently did not lack for friends at school or in the village. The role model which he adopted was that of the holy man, reinforced by an often ruthless desire to train himself physically as well as mentally. His precocious determination was wondered at. It is one of the great strengths of India that its myriad villages can so often give birth to religious heroes who become reformers and activators on a wider stage.

In later days, reminiscing, he remarked:

'Village folk hardly understand what is *jap* or meditation. Because I remained sitting for long hours, people used to wonder – what does he do, remaining seated, doing nothing? Is he an idiot? In truth, It was very simple, I did not understand the world or its ways. Besides that *one thing*, there was nothing else in my head.'

So there was something special about the child Binode: a strong will, a fascination with self-training, a predisposition to the life of vision. But it was a life played out in a large, rather prosperous family, amid the rice-fields, ponds and rivers of green Bengal. He was unconsciously preparing himself for wider work in the restless years of the early twentieth-century Raj.

2
EARLY STRUGGLES
AND SCHOOLDAYS

From his early days the young Binode was drawn to spiritual pursuits and a kind of ascetic athleticism. In 1913 when he was coming up to his seventeenth birthday, and not long before he left school, his headmaster noted a kind of detachment in Binode: 'He would be seen with an exercise book and lead pencil and sometimes a book, sitting on a back bench by a big window, giving the impression that he had come to school just to sit for a moment on his journey somewhere else.' From the age of 13 he had been practising *tapas*, or austerities – a rigorous self-disciplining. Indeed he was consumed with a number of themes which take us to the heart of one main form of Hindu spirituality – *tapas* and yoga, the *brahmacharya* ideal, the possibility of becoming a *guru* or teacher, and a concern for the formless *Brahman* as well as the personal God. But Binode was also drawn to other themes which were significant for his later political and social work: athleticism; the reform and protection of the Hindu tradition; and the struggle against the British.

We can imagine the religiously precocious and somewhat eccentric lad, sitting motionless in the thatched outhouse which he had taken over, long into the night, perhaps at times concentrating somewhat absently on his homework, almost oblivious most of the time to the sounds around him in the Bengali night, the murmur of voices from the family house, the distant music in the rambling village, the last calls of the water birds. Not all the villagers could understand his passion for sitting still, nor was his family at ease with his austere diet – rice, perhaps with a few vegetables, and the water the rice was boiled in. He was independent in spirit and wanted to be independent in body too. Despite the rigours of his regime, he was strong and burly. His body filled out as he grew to be a youth; and his face was round and flanked by long, luxuriant hair. He was certainly not the picture of the emaciated yogi that one finds in sculptures of Shiva and the Buddha. But Binode had ambitions similar to those of the Buddha, to achieve some kind of spiritual emancipation.

The *tapas* which he performed corresponded to an ancient theme in the Indian religious tradition. Literally the word means 'heat'. It refers to the heat which the practitioner of austerities is traditionally supposed to generate in his own body as his power increases. For the Hindu austerity does not empty you: it fills you with power, and that can threaten even the gods. This old mythic theme is seen in the representations of Shiva as the great divine ascetic, naked, with matted hair, smeared with ashes and wearing a garland of skulls, sitting on a tigerskin in deep meditation, protected by a cobra canopy, beneath a sacred tree. This representation goes back to the ancient Indus Valley civilisation of three thousand years ago. Its somewhat fierce and dramatic portrayal of Shiva can startle and frighten us: but its essential message is the power of the divine and the power of austerity to draw on God's creative energy in concentrated form, ready to blaze forth in splendour.

At a human level, it was a mode whereby the young Binode could focus his own, growing powers. To say that by *tapasya* (the practise of *tapas*) he produced literal heat is to misunderstand the spiritual character of the exercise. It is true that yogis often experience sweating and a kind of hot, stinging sensation in the early stages of their self-control, as the energy known as *kundalini* (imagined as a coiled serpent at the base of the spine) begins to rise up the central column of the subtle body. Whatever we make of such descriptions there is no doubt that those who practise yogic self-control can feel higher and higher states of consciousness which ultimately suffuse the whole of their being with bliss. Later

Binode was to say about this period of austerity, and especially the time from 1913 to 1916 just after he left school: 'There was fire in my head that could be felt twenty inches above me'.

He was certainly pursuing a role in which his perception of his own direction in life was becoming clearer. He sensed, increasingly, that he had some kind of divine mission. Even in his early teens he felt the challenge of the Buddha's example. But he had much less interest than might have been expected in sitting at the feet of other teachers. He seems to have been convinced of his own powers and abilities at self-control and meditation – and these were formidable – and this confidence made him think that he could follow his own path to some kind of final insight. He thus became more convinced that he was predetermined to be a great teacher. His early life was a rigorous preparation for this destiny.

By 1909, as he sensed the coming of adulthood, he looked to the old ideals embedded in Indian tradition. He determined on a path of strict *brahmacharya*. He later came to be known as Brahmachari Binode during this part of his life, until he took the title of *Acharya* (Teacher) in 1916.

Literally *brahmacharya* means 'divine living' or '*brahman* living'. A multiplicity of ideas find echoes in this very word, lying beneath the surface meaning that it is the student period in Indian tradition when the young man serves his teacher and preserves chastity, waiting to go on to the next stage of life, that of marriage and being a householder. The echoes are those of *brahman*, that divine or holy power which is implicit and discharged through the sacrificial ritual of the beginningless past and which also inhabits the brahmin who, rich in this power, can conduct the ritual and bring divine blessings on those who offer the sacrifice. But it is a divine power which also pervades the whole universe. The universe itself is a manifestation of cosmic sacrament, a mysterious unfolding of God's ritual and magical outreach, as if the whole world were a vast sacrifice in which sacral power is mediated to all beings. *Brahman* in the Upanishads, however, is more than all this. It is also identified with the eternal Self which lies within the heart of every person, the light that lights each living being from within. So the yogi, reaching inward through self-control to attain the deepest insight and consciousness of his own nature, is also voyaging into *brahman*. Such echoes connect with the sexual significance of *brahmacharya*. The student in traditional Vedic lore is one who learns the secret and mysterious truths about God from his teacher; but he also practises continence. Binode attached very great importance to this and tried to influence his fellow schoolboys in this.

The Indian tradition has never been prudish in sexual matters. Although there may be reserve in social behaviour between the sexes, the religious and other texts and traditions have never been afraid to discuss openly the physiology of sex and the spiritual meaning of the various procreative processes. In particular there is a well-discussed concept of the significance of semen. It is the vital power. It is human power in concentrated form. The *Bṛhadāranyaka* Upanishad states:

'Of created things earth is the essence; of earth moisture; of moisture plants; of plants flowers; of flowers fruit; of fruit man; of man semen.'

Binode thus saw the importance of celibacy during this critical period of transition in his life. As a dedicated *brahmachari* he regarded the strictest observance of complete chastity as the basis of his whole code of behaviour. He thought of the male seed as the source of power and so retaining it was essential to physical as well as spiritual wellbeing. He ascribed his own power and health to this practice. Of this he was utterly convinced, as witness his own rather passionate words:

'Male seed is the vital energy; it is the elixir of life; it is energy crystallised; it is the nectar of immortality; it is the concrete form of manhood and manliness; nay, it is divine!'

We can see in this quite a different attitude from that which is prevalent in the West, or was at least in Binode's day. Here chastity was also praised, before marriage and, by Catholics, among priests, nuns, and others. But in this there was a fear of sex as riddled with desire, concupiscence and the associations of sin. The Hindu attitude is more down-to-earth and at the same time spiritual. Semen as power is not to be wasted. And power can be diverted to a higher end. It was their conservation of semen that gave the *rishis* or seers of old their power to draw men and women to them. There is almost a natural magnetism of the celibate ascetic. In him there is retained that vital essence which animates not only the individual but the whole universe.

Binode would cite scripture to this effect. He began to try to influence his school companions in this practice. It is a hard ideal to follow but it later became a central engine of his whole movement. As for his school companions, they could assist themselves by watching their diet – for certain kinds of food, such as onions, have always been thought to arouse sexual desire – by taking frequent exercise and by practising meditation regularly. He adopted that classical ideal of a sound mind in a sound body, *mens sana in corpore sano*.

Thus he saw his striving for purity and insight as meshed into the building up of his own spiritual and mental strength. He was single-minded in his pursuit of self-control and of improving his body. Even on those numerous feast days when the village celebrated the major religious festivals he did not, like the other lads, fill himself with the gaudy, sticky confectionery that sweetens the young Hindu's life. He tried physical exercises, such as working out with two heavy wooden clubs, swinging their 140 pounds' weight two thousand times to strengthen his muscles. He took part in school games, being much in demand in particular in the tug of war because of his weight and strength. There are various anecdotes that have come down about his prowess.

There is the story of a Muslim who used to bully some of the Bajitpur villagers and terrorise Hindu girls so that they were afraid to go out alone. Binode heard about this. One

23

evening as the sun was going down he was taking a stroll by a village stream, along the grassy bank, when he became aware of someone lurking in the shadows behind him. He somehow had the feeling that this was the bully in question.

He turned on him and said: 'Are you the man who is harassing people?'

The man replied: 'I'll do what I like. I'm not afraid of you or anybody else.'

Binode suddenly leapt on him, grabbed him by the leg, flung him to the ground and pinned him down. The man realised he had met his match, and promised to refrain from his bullying. In later life Binode was equally fearless and considered that having spiritual interests did not mean being physically weak. The incident was the forerunner of his organisation of self-defence parties to protect Hindu women and others from gangs in East Bengal. It also spread the reputation he had begun to acquire of great physical strength.

So one day a group of five young men came to his home, with the idea of testing his physical strength against theirs, of which they were proud. At first Binode did not want to accept their challenge. He said he had wrestled with the bully in order to teach him a lesson, and not to show off his strength, and he was not going to do that now. But his visitors at least wanted a demonstration of how he had worsted the ruffian. So Binode in fact repeated his act, suddenly setting on them one by one and hurling them to the ground. It was a good proof of his power and energy, and the five had bruises to remind them of that proof.

His concern for strict *brahmacharya* led him to try to help his fellow students to overcome temptation. He found that they were willing to talk to him more than to their parents and elders. In particular he tried to assist them in overcoming the habit of masturbation: this was something which greatly disturbed him. From this his advice spread to other things. Here we have an example of Binode as a youthful guru for youths, a friend and equal, yet also someone with sincere beliefs and great self-control and power. Thus his fellow students would ask him for the sort of advice that they could not easily get from others about the things that worried them. Why was it hard for them to concentrate on their studies? Why did they feel so sleepy or lazy, why were they weak, why did they look pale, why could they not retain semen, why did they have nocturnal emissions, and so on? He became a centre of advice in himself. The young would come to him, especially after school hours, at weekends and during holidays. One can imagine this village 'confessor' in his thatched hut, gaining a reputation for wisdom; a strange lad, but a powerful one; a precociously religious person but sympathetic and without reserve. He was a leader too, for the student community was restless with vague and exciting ambition to struggle against the hated rulers of the land, and their thoughts turned to revolution and Hindu self-improvement. Such restlessness was especially infectious with the coming of war in 1914. The young were beginning to learn from other national movements – hearing and reading about Garibaldi and Mazzini, the Russian revolutionaries secretly conspiring against the Tsar, and the new generation of Hindu and Muslim nationalist leaders. Thus did the vast imponderables of the outside world reach their fingers into the minds of the youth of Bajitpur. The battles and struggles of faraway Europe and the restlessness of many beyond Bengal were to be reflected in the streams and ponds of the green Bengali countryside. Young men's fancies turned to thoughts not only of love but also of war, revolvers and clandestine bombs. Sarajevos were to be enacted in Chittagong and Calcutta. Bombs were to be set off beneath the carriages of the proud British officials. Some of the young followers that had come to gather round Binode, now 18 years old, had joined a secret revolutionary society, the Anushilan Samiti, and began to acquire pistols. They were inspired with a kind of reckless courage and were willing to die if caught. Binode did not discourage them from their patriotism but neither did he think that Indian freedom was to be simply won by shooting policemen and British officials.

One evening two of his young revolutionary friends visited

him, and Binode had either knowledge or a premonition that they were being followed and watched by the police. Urgently he told them to get rid of their guns. He took the revolvers and handed them to his sister in the main house. The police came to his outhouse and searched it, without result. To their questions about the names of his two visitors, Binode replied: 'Their names? We never ask our visitors' names. They requested blessings and went away.'

The police could do little but they were suspicious. Binode was a marked man. Later that year he was arrested and held in gaol, in solitary confinement, for the best part of a month. No specific charge was made against him, and in due course he was released, at the request of Babu Ambika Charan Mazumdar, an influential family friend and one-time President of the Indian Congress. Without this intervention he might have been transferred to another prison and held indefinitely. His experience in gaol was not too bad for him, for as he pointed out afterwards he simply meditated in his cell much as he was accustomed to in his outhouse.

He sympathised with the aspirations of his young friends but he considered that India would never become free and take its proper place as a proud nation, well-endowed both physically and spiritually, until its people had acquired discipline. In particular the youth of the nation had to be built up to be tough and insightful in matters of both religion and secular life. Binode dreamed of national liberation, and he saw his own destiny as a holy person in the making in the context of this national struggle. Much later he was to write:

'In order to guard and develop your personality in this great battlefield of life you should strictly observe . . . celibacy and continence. The manliness and heroism of the Sangha-monk lie in the observance of *brahmacharya*. For want of *brahmacharya* the whole nation has become lifeless and has been accompanied by idleness, inertia, lethargy, slumber and indifference. No trace of hope, no aspiration, no display of energy and effort is observable in the life of the nation at present. The entire country is sunk

26

in a slough of despondency and despair. In order to remove this sad state of affairs it is very necessary to inculcate a vigorous influence of self-control in the hearts of the people and thus awaken and enliven them with the vibration of life and energy.'

It should be noted that there was nothing withdrawn about this asceticism: it was to gear energy to the this-worldly fight for independence and a Hindu renaissance. We shall later observe something of the effects of the *brahma-charya* movement which he founded in 1927.

So Binode felt himself to be following a path of great struggle to perfect himself as an instrument of the Divine Being for his life's work, which he foresaw as having to do with a regeneration of the Hindu spirit in the context of the national struggle. The methods he set himself were well-defined. As one of his companions described it, the young Brahmanchari set himself tasks like the following:

'This much shall I eat; so much shall I sleep; I shall not eat or sleep before I complete so many prayers; I shall not touch any luxurious food; I shall not use shoes or jackets; I shall not sleep more than two hours and that too lying half way; on the way to and from school I shall keep looking downwards for this whole month; next Sunday I shall remain sitting in one pose for six hours at one stretch, then twice a week, then thrice a week I shall not sleep at all and will spend the nights in meditation; next month once a week, the following month twice a week and the month after thrice a week I shall keep silence for twenty four hours, and so on.'

An example of how this minute self-control worked out is as follows. The headmaster of his school tells how during the Shiva festival he, another teacher, a Sanskrit pandit and Binode decided to keep the vigil for the whole night. Binode had the responsibility for collecting the flowers, *bel* leaves and other necessities (*bel* or *bilva* is a tree with threefold

27

leaves somewhat like clover, which is sacred to Shiva and whose wood is not to be used for fuel save by Brahmins). They sang hymns and did *puja* or worship the whole night, with occasional breaks when they would go outside the temple. But Binode remained sitting in the same spot without moving an inch. As the master said, 'Clad in white clothes he looked like a snow-covered Shiva.' Gradually the headmaster got to know him well and despite the distance of their ages they became intimates and spent much time discussing the condition of the youth of Bengal. About this Binode was sometimes despairing.

He regretted deeply what he saw as their lack of manliness. How could the weak work for the country? What is the point, he asked, of clamouring for 'Home Rule! Home Rule! Home Rule!' The students would have to be taught hardship and to 'swing back to India's ancient ideal'. He saw the struggle both of his own life and for independence in terms of a kind of war. It was necessary for the young people to train themselves as if for battle. As a soldier is always on alert in the battlefield so should the spiritual practitioner be. He should be ready to cut through his enemies with the sword of discrimination and of indifference to the world. A spiritual person, or *sadhaka*, should acquire strength.

Binode's thinking on these matters even as a youth incorporated three key concepts of the tradition: *viveka* or discrimination; *vairagya* or equanimity, indifference to the world, and *sadhana*. Traditionally, discrimination means insight into the difference between what is eternal and what is not eternal. Very often this is interpreted to mean that the person with discrimination has immediate knowledge through yogic experience of the transcendent as impersonal. This is often labelled the '*Brahman* without qualities', the ineffable Absolute lying behind or beyond the personal Lord of everyday worship and prayer. As for equanimity, this does not mean being cut off from the world; it means being indifferent to pain and pleasure and the good or bad things which may happen to you. But the typical saint of the Indian tradition, whether Hindu, Buddhist or Jain, is still moved to

28

act on behalf of others who suffer, while preserving his or her equanimity in the face of both disaster and success. In his later life the Acharya was to display both equanimity and moral and religious concern. Because of such detachment, however, in regard to personal interests the *sadhaka* or searcher for the ultimate goes beyond the duties and immediate worries of ordinary society. He who has achieved the higher life is the *sadhu* or holy man who lives in a sense at the margins of society, transcending caste and the usual requirements of the law or *dharma*. In transcending everyday life such a *sadhu* however may make a tremendous contribution to the life of ordinary people by providing a bridge between the impermanent and the Eternal, between daily life and the higher Reality.

During his schooldays Binode was already practising to be a *sadhu* himself. But although his self-training was the core of his life, he nevertheless continued with outer activities. He needed to go to school, where he did not distinguish himself academically although he did win the award for good conduct. His Bengali writing ability was good and foreshadowed his later fluency and vivid style. He enriched his Bengali with many Sanskrit expressions, and was fairly good at Sanskrit also. He knew the language somewhat through the sacred books and the recitations of Brahmins, since Sanskrit was of course used in the traditional rituals. His English was less sure, and there was little chance to use it in rural Bengal. It was a language used by magistrates and others involved in administration and higher education but it had little purchase on Bajitpur. Bengali was the daily tongue, frequently laced with Sanskrit. It is as if modern Italians used as much Latin as possible in their speech; for Bengali was a daughter of the middle Indic of ancient times and itself a close vernacular relative of Sanskrit. But although Binode encouraged his fellow students to do well in examinations, his ambitions and vocation lay elsewhere.

Despite his strange detachment and absorption in matters of the spirit, he was well-liked at school. If teased for his absent-mindedness he would ignore any taunts. He took part in some of the more strenuous games and was, as we have seen, an adviser to his fellows in intimate matters. He and those he gathered around him engaged in social work and would go round the classrooms at school trying to collect some money for the desperately poor students. By night his group would go to help the elderly and destitute, fetching medicines for them, nursing them if need be and feeding them if they could not cook for themselves. His group even formed a voluntary firebrigade for Bajitpur and its surroundings. They also helped during cholera outbreaks: on one occasion Binode nursed a poor Muslim hit by the disease for seven days and nights. Thus he gathered a loyal following and despite his somewhat detached manner was outgoing to others and popular as well as inspiring a spirit of social service in his fellows. Some were revolutionaries, as we have noted. He never cut himself off from them for he approved their aims if not their methods. He worried about them and the dangers of their being led astray. And he worried too about the more frivolous and worldly students who could not follow his strict example of chastity and social service.

His schooldays came to an end when he was 17. There was no question of his going on to college. He had rather different ambitions, which were now to become a matter of urgency for him. In 1913–14 he embarked on the next major steps in his religious pilgrimage with some help from the headmaster, who became a firm friend and spiritual helper.

Although he was active and influential among his peers, much of his most intense life was spent in his outhouse and from about 1910 he kept vigil there every night. Later he said that he did not sleep for six years; and (although this may sound incredible) during this period he denied himself rest until he might attain final illumination. There is little doubt that he trained himself to make do with less and less sleep. If he did sleep it was in the sitting position of meditation. Whatever the details of his self-mastery in this respect it is clear that he was incredibly persistent and vigorous in his relentless drive to perfect his austerity and self-control. If there can be boy-geniuses in music, why not boy-geniuses of the ascetic life? This period of his life extended beyond his school days, and we shall soon see how they culminated in greater heights of spiritual experience. But one wonders in all this what the villagers of Bajitpur thought of this exceptional young man as he grew from childhood to manhood during his days at the high school. Perhaps the typical villager thought as follows.

'He is a fine-looking boy, that third son of Bishnu Charan Das and Sumati Devi: but he is a strange one too. All those hours he spends in that little thatched cottage in their yard: they say he just sits there as though he is asleep, but with his eyes open. What is the good of sitting so long, right into the night, doing nothing? They say he sometimes rises up and floats above the ground. It could be, for he dresses like a saint, and we can remember there have been all those stories of his knowledge and visions even as a little child. Some of the lads in the village thought he was soft, but he soon gave them their come-uppance: he can wrestle as well as anyone. Remember how he dealt with that ruffian who was molesting our girls? He is a strong-looking young fellow, but he has a faraway look in his eyes. How is he so strong when all he eats is rice and boiled potatoes or *dal* occasionally? Maybe the rumours are right, and he has a divine destiny. Some whisper, including his mother, that he is divine: a descent of Vishnu perhaps, or an incarnation of Shiva. Fancy such a mighty thing in Bajitpur of all places! If you peep in through the cracks in his hut at night you can see him there, in the light of a small lamp, and there is such a look on his face, as if he saw right through the wall, right through the village, right through everything, to the divine sphere itself! Aye, he is a strange lad. But he never causes trouble and everyone respects him, it seems. Remember how he helped, together with his schoolmates, during last year's flood? And the fire in those huts at the other end of the village? And how he helps some of the poor old folk? There is nothing wrong with him. He is a good young man, and so eloquent about the need to strengthen India. He wants us all to be free. I wonder, though, how he will make out when he leaves the high

31

school? Will he become a teacher of some kind: but how? He does not want to go to college. I think, though, that the world will hear a lot of this Binode. He calls himself Brahmachari. I wouldn't be surprised if he will take off from here. He is a fearless one, that Binode. They say he sits by the cremation ground and handles skulls. And if there's a woman with you he never looks at you. He doesn't even look at the women of his family. He is always looking down at the ground when he goes off to school and comes back at night. He doesn't enjoy himself like the other boys. He's so pious. I've never seen anyone so rapt in the Temple, so attentive during the feast days. Some day he will be a saint, perhaps. He has that look. May God bless him. May he bless us.'

Such thoughts about Binode may well have reflected the attitude of many of the villagers. They did not regret Binode's influence on their sons. They drew ideals from him, which is perhaps why the headmaster could seem, in his last days at school, to share his pastoral oversight of the pupils with the young student who had a glint of God in his eyes and a deep love of India in his heart.

If the villagers thought he was going to leave the village, they were right and they were wrong. The village was destined to be the spiritual hub of the movement he was to found and the scene of a great spiritual turning point in his life. But before that he had to go away first. He had yearnings which were to lead him nearer the completion of his *brahma-charya* and the end of his religious beginning.

32

3
SPIRITUAL EMANCIPATION

Towards the end of his school days Binode began to look more broadly at his future. He told Birendra Lal Bhattacharya, the headmaster, that he would like to become a monk. But the headmaster became worried at this idea. There were many false teachers around, and there was a danger of falling into the wrong environment. He had no doubt that the young man was a great yogi. But also he was involved indirectly in political action, for he had remarked to the headmaster that unless he became a monk he would not be able to help the revolutionaries among the students. Birendra thought it best for Binode to go and take initiation from his own preceptor, Baba Gambhiranathji of Gorakhpur. He suggested this course to Binode, who gave him an odd reply. 'Can man become *guru*, sir?'

Perhaps Binode was thinking that only a divine being could become a true *guru*. Had he not himself, through his childhood visions, come into contact with the highest preceptor of all? Moreover he had on his own fought great battles within his soul, and had achieved great feats of *tapasya*. He had not had the guidance of a *guru* in all this. He was in effect his own preceptor. And so he may have thought it unnecessary to bow before any human being, or accept someone else's authority.

But he was open-minded about the headmaster's suggestion. He had come to respect Birendra's judgement, as a person truly involved in spiritual matters. Increasingly they were becoming friends, not separated by the usual gulf that divides the master from the schoolboy. Some time later he

33

came to the headmaster and said, with a broad smile, 'Be it so, sir. I will go. I wish to be initiated.' So the two of them planned the trip to Gorakhpur, far to the West, in United Provinces (now Uttar Pradesh). There, on the day after the new moon in October 1913, the young *Brahmachari* received initiation from the famous yogi, Gambhiranathji.

The teacher had been kind and warm to him and had said that it was scarcely necessary for him to be ordained or, at least, not to enter fully the monastic life. This also tallied with the tradition that only those aged 50 or above should enter into ordination as a *sannyasi*. At the time when the ceremony was due to take place, Binode sat apart under a tree in a tangled grove near by the *Math* or monastery, thinking that if Gambhiranath were a person of true insight he would initiate him separately. His wish was granted, and the *guru*, unprompted, gave Binode a special initiation, which brought about enormous consequences for the young *brahmachari* – a sort of explosion of trance.

In going to the Gorukhpur *Math* (monastery), Binode was conforming to the ancient Hindu pattern of learning from a *guru*: but it would have been more normal to have had such a teacher during his early period of practising yoga. The initiation is a vital ingredient in the tradition, in which it is thought that a secret handing on of knowledge can be ritually conveyed from the teacher to the student, from the *guru* to the *chela* or disciple. This goes with the vow of obedience which the student makes to his *guru*. There was now a period in the young man's life which was directly under the guidance of the famous holy man, first for eight months in Gorukhpur, and then for a time in Banaras, when he maintained contact with Yogi Gambhiranathji.

The period after initiation was filled with almost continuous meditation. He dwelt outside the monastery, and, unlike other disciples of the *Guru*, did not occupy himself with practical tasks such as cleaning, washing, cooking, sweeping, tidying the grounds and the like. The *Guru* would have to send someone out to bring Binode in to eat from time to time: of his own volition he simply stayed in his prolonged state of meditation. His lack of activity of a 'useful' kind annoyed a fellow *brahmachari*, Kalinath. But eventually, when he came to see the continuity and depth of Binode's religious practice, he relented. Another *sadhu* at the monastery came across Binode early one morning in the monks' graveyard which he used for meditation, and also observed his ability with the heavy clubs with which he continued to practice. He brought him food to sustain him. The practice of meditating in a graveyard or a burning ground was already familiar to Binode and was a well-known tradition in Indian spirituality, going back to the time of the Buddha and beyond.

After eight months of yoga and self-mortification in Gorukhpur, Binode sought the *Guru*'s permission to go on to the holy city of Banaras, also in Uttar Pradesh. So it was in the latter half of 1914 that the young man came to the famous city beside the looping Ganges, sacred river of the Hindus.

For those who have not been there it is hard to convey the impact of Banaras (or more properly Varanasi: it is also known by its ancient name of Kasi). It is set on a sweeping curve of the Ganges lined with bathing steps (the *ghats*) and a cluster of temples. On the opposite bank there is open land and further up the palace of the maharajah and a tangle of other buildings. Even in Binode's day there would be crowds of people pouring into the city from its five railway stations. And the streets were dense with the confusion of all kinds of traffic. Beyond the main city in one direction was the cantonment, heart of the British administration and of military and social life. In the other direction, facing the maharajah's palace, was empty land (now occupied by Banaras Hindu University, in part the brain child of Pandit Madan Mohan Malaviya and Annie Besant). Then as now the city was a busy place of pilgrimage. The *ghats* were crowded with holy men, white-clad widows and throngs of devotees. In the morning as the sun was beginning to rise many would be there in the healing waters ready to greet him.

Along the *ghats* were walls, balconies and small palaces, interspersed with peaked temples, climbing gold roofs, plat-

35

forms for teachers, and more temples of every size. There were boats, curved and carved, laden with passengers and produce; and the lazy smoke curling up from where the dead were burned; and capacious umbrellas fixed upon the *ghats* to shield the faithful. There were all manner of holy men and women and pious lay people, and all manner of places where they sang fervent hymns to the gods, such as Ganesh, Shiva, the avatars of Vishnu and many other saviours and heavenly lords. The scene was overshadowed, too, by the great mosque of Aurangzeb. Very few temples were old because until the sixteenth century and beyond, Muslim piety and vigour had razed the sanctuaries and idols of the profane Hindus. But Banaras survived and kept its Hindu stamp; the very air was pervaded by prayer and incense. It was impossible not to feel in the slanting sunlight of evening or in the misty milkiness of the holy dawn, the presence of the Lord and lords, God and the goddesses, the marrow and power of the sacred land and its holy Spirit. It was impossible not to sense the unheard sound of old philosophies. It was to this city then that the young Binode, like so many before him back to the Buddha's time and even earlier, came wandering in that monsoon season of 1914 (when in distant Europe the guns began to thunder, presaging new weaknesses in the Empire).

We do not know much about the *brahmachari's* stay in Banaras. It seems that when he arrived there he was already coming down with a fever. By good fortune he somehow met an old lady who was looking for a lodger to stay with her because she was frightened of living alone. She wanted someone who would not leave her alone after dark. Her house was by the Ashi Ghat, near where one of the two small streams (Varana and Ashi) that give Banaras its name flows into the Ganges. Binode spent hours and days at the Harischandra Ghat, which is used for cremation, where he would meditate on death. When the *ghat* was crowded he would continue his contemplative exercises on the Ashi Ghat. But his regime accentuated his fever, and he became seriously ill. If it had not been for the devoted care of his landlady he might not

have lived. During his illness he had visions of Gambhiranath, who encouraged him and took him spiritually to the
major pilgrimage centres of India. Binode felt that he was
thus accomplishing what many take years to perform. Similarly when the *Guru* told him of the most difficult and
advanced yogic feats, Binode felt that he already had performed these inwardly. At any rate, when he was better he
mastered these exercises in twenty-one days instead of the
twenty-one years it is usually reputed to take to complete
them. After two months he left Banaras. It was as if despite
his sickness he had made contact with the earthly point of
intersection between the Brahman world and this world. He
left behind him the bright silky evenings of the *ghats* and the
smoky sunrises and returned to the greener fields and glades
of the Bengali countryside. He was back in Bajitpur.

Banaras had intensified his home experience. The Harischandra Ghat was a powerful prototype of the burning
ground not far from his home, where he would often go by
night to meditate. Even as a young boy he had sought out the
skull of one of his brother's sons, who had died in infancy. He
would handle it as a real, gruesome, striking testimony to the
impermanence of human reality, and a means for becoming
dispassionate. The cremation ground was a gymnasium of
dispassion, as his thatched cottage and the Ashi Ghat were
each a gymnasium of discrimination.

When he arrived home his meditation became more
intense. He was a master of *nirvikalpa samadhi* – the deepest
imageless trance in which the mystic attains unity with the
formless *Brahman*. On one occasion he confined himself to a
loft in his parents' house for twenty-one days without eating;
on another occasion it was fourteen days and again he ate
nothing except a few spoonfuls of *bel* juice. There were
other, similarly long plunges into trance. Once, after seven
days in the loft, he came out with a high fever. His family
called the doctor from the local charitable dispensary, a
certain Dr Bharat Bhushan Chakravarty, who examined him
and found that he had a temperature (unprecedented) of
107. The doctor thought that even an elephant would

succumb to such heat. But was it not somehow yogically induced? At any rate by the next day the fever had gone. A week passed and he decided to fast for another fortnight, except for *bel* juice, which his mother would leave outside the door (poor apprehensive mother: she tried to cheat by leaving some fruit there as well, but he was not tempted to take it). When he came out he seemed to be as strong as ever. This at any rate was the testimony of his family: and it may confirm the notion that the complete bliss of *samadhi* which Binode declared that he experienced had a transformative effect on the body also. He was richly suffused with the blinding perception of Godhead.

It is not quite clear what the sequence of events was during this period between his return from Banaras until his final achievement of enlightenment and the closure of this phase of self-mortification. While he was in Bajitpur he continued with his activities of rousing his youthful followers to greater feats of social action and deeper appreciation of Hinduism's spiritual heritage. He often took his younger brother to his night sessions in the cremation ground, to warn others who might otherwise be shocked and frightened by the still, ghostly figure of the young and burly yogi, shining white in the darkness of the hot night, his *dhoti* and robe wrapped closely round him.

But there were occasions in the year after his visit to Banaras when he went off to various places – on pilgrimage to Chandranath Hill, Sitakundu and the Jagatpur monastery, as well as to the port city of Chittagong. It is not certain why he went on these journeys. One possibility is that he was seeking a place to plant his 'seat' or *asana*, the spot where he might achieve the complete enlightenment for which he was striving.

For there was no doubt that in all the six years of his fierce *tapas* and self-control he was eagerly, indeed almost impatiently, seeking to achieve a final sense of divine mission, an enlightenment which would confirm his breakthrough into the highest life of which humanity is capable. He felt himself like a Buddha, and a Buddha who also was his own teacher

38

and master, for all the help that he received from his famous *Guru*. At the beginning of his period of struggle, in 1909 or 1910, when he was still only 13 or 14 years old, he reflected on the example of Gautama himself and his famous vow:

> 'Let my body dry on this seat, my skin and bone and flesh be destroyed, yet I shall not leave my seat without achieving that rare *bodhi*. The great mountains may change their positions, the world may merge in space, the planets may fall from their orbits, the oceans may dry up, but none can move me from my seat under this tree.'

It was a frantic challenge but Binode was visionary enough to take courage from the Buddha's example. The trip to Gorakhpur, the initiation, the sojourn in Banaras, the wanderings to some of the holy places of Bengal – these all were part of the mosaic of a restless pursuit of final experience. But in the last resort he came back to his native Bajitpur. He knew where he could be both at home and homeless, both within society and outside it. The next and in some ways the most central part of his life was about to unfold. We have in all this to imagine a person who saw adventure in inwardness, joy in self-conquest, battles in the struggle against demonic forces and the hankerings of the flesh, discoveries in trances, supreme joys in the floodlights within the skull, thrills in the climb towards liberation. His life was in his own eyes an adventure-saga of yogic experience and sensations of insight, devotion, godliness and the supreme emptiness of the ultimate. He took with great seriousness the practical side of the ancient tradition. His ambition, though inward-pointing, was concrete.

He resolved the question of where to plant his *asana* close to home. Just opposite the cremation ground which he frequented, across a branch of the stream which wound its way through the village and through the green meadow into the river Kumar, was a tangle of jungle. It was a dangerous and haunting place. In this swampy nest of bushes and half-rotten trees and creepers, there was an ancient altar, where once a year a congregation would gather to worship Bana-Durga, a form of the fierce Goddess so much revered in Bengal.

He had, after all, received an experiential visitation from the Goddess. The place was close to the cremation ground which had seen so many of his night vigils. It was close to the village, and yet on the other hand it was wild. It was both far, psychologically, from ordinary living, and yet near as the crow flies. One reason for its sad and desolate condition was that it was usually flooded each year as the mighty Padma River rose and the Kumar and its little tributaries overflowed their banks, swamping the difficult patch of jungle. It was here that the *Brahmachari* determined to establish his *asana*, his sitting-place, and reach at last, he hoped, the final illumination which would round off the six or more years of austerity that he had undertaken. It would be the spot from which his life's mission could radiate. He would here receive the power and enlightenment which would enable him to fulfil his destiny and help India in its enfeebled and chaotic condition.

So Binode had a platform built there with a hermitage on it. Ultimately this was to become the chief ceremonial centre of the movement. It gradually transformed the swamp into a delightful glade. It was here on the full moon day of the month of *Magh*, in February 1916 by the Western calendar, that he was the focus of a religious celebration. Both his youthful followers and the local villagers gathered to chant the name of the Lord. It was during the culmination of the feast that he sat beneath a *kadamba* tree and felt himself enter into the great illumination which he had been working and waiting for all these years. It was as if the spark which Gambhiranath had cast into his inner consciousness through the ordination had finally blazed out in a great light. Binode felt himself consumed by the Divine Being. Indeed he felt that he had realised that oneness with *Brahman* which is such a prominent theme in the Hindu tradition, from the Upanishads onwards.

We can imagine that scene near the heart of Bajitpur. The

sight of the white-clad Binode, seated beneath the auspicious tree in the lotus posture, for all the world like a latter-day Buddha; near him the crowd of villagers and pious youths who chanted the names of God, and recalled the divine Durga; the earth platform decorated with blossoms beneath the creepers and trees of the patch of warm jungle which Binode had chosen as his new home-from-home; the great white moon glancing through the leaves and branches; the atmosphere of devotion to God and loyalty to the now increasingly famous young yogi and *sannyasi* of Bajitpur – this scene was the outer covering of what Binode felt to be going on within his soul.

Can that be imagined also? I think so, for there is the testimony of other mystics, saints and philosophers of religious traditions both Eastern and Western. Perhaps the ordinary person can only be dimly aware of the consciousness of a saint or yogin, but we can at least have imaginative intimations of what may have happened to Binode at that auspicious place in February 1916. He spoke of it as illumination. But there are differing kinds of illumination. For the young man (he was still only 20 years old), the light which flooded his soul could have seemed like the enlightenment experience of the Buddha: but such experiences are typically not discursive. There is no time for thinking, nor is there a desire, in such higher bliss, to get entangled in even the deepest thoughts. There is indeed no time; as the poet and mystic Henry Vaughan put it 'I saw Eternity the other night'. We must imagine that the yogi Binode, already adept at the imageless trance to which his own yogic teacher had shown him the path, was aware of a higher sense, not just of that dazzling emptiness in the very centre of his being, but of a divine radiance within. Was it possible in such awareness to distinguish his self from the Self, his soul from *Brahman*? Surely, afterwards he must have recalled that famous Upanishadic saying (*Muṇḍaka Upanishad* 3:2:9): '*Sa yo ha vai tat paramam brahma veda brahmaiva bhavati*' (He who knows that highest *Brahman* Being becomes *Brahman* himself). Binode had that final overwhelming sensation of

41

being merged in God, in being fused with the bright light of the Holy Power which pervades and sustains all this universe.

There may have been something else at the edge of this consciousness of glory. The sounds of those villagers singing hymns to the Lord and the murmurs of prayer and devotion which suffused the Bengali night on that auspicious moonlit occasion, may have triggered in him the feeling, later to be expressed, that he was not destined to be like those silent Buddhas and holy recluses for whom the world ceases to have meaning. Rather he was aware that the divine consciousness which he experienced in himself was driving him outwards and onwards. He was predestined to act in the world, and was to see his mission as helping the poor and leading Hindus towards a rediscovery of the essence and majesty of the tradition. In short, his direction was not only inwards – the path of the hermit yogi. He sensed his identity with the Absolute in this vision of enlightenment, and yet this did not make the world of suffering people unreal.

There has been debate as to whether he was a Monist or a Dualist. It should be pointed out that these terms have to be seen in their Hindu context. The Monist or Non-Dualist position (whose primary exponent was of course the great Shankara) took with utmost seriousness those texts, including the one we have quoted above, which state the identity of the eternal self within a person and the Divine Being or Brahman. If indeed my essential 'I' is identical with the Divine, then all individuals likewise contain the same eternal divine essence. There is only one divine reality. All else is merely ephemeral; it is all illusion, *māyā*. For Shankara, all the things which we experience at the level of ordinary existence are ultimately insignificant. Knowledge of them belongs to the lower level of truth. The worship of God, since it implies duality, is likewise merely secondary, without ultimate meaning, useful for exalting the ignorant but not representing at all the final truth about Reality.

By contrast, Dualists, whether of the strict variety represented by the Dvaita school of Madhva, or more moderate and ingenious as in the theology of Ramanuja, stress the difference between the worshipper and the Lord. They see individuals as recognising their difference from the Lord who created them and who is the guider and shaper of their destinies. Both the Monist and the Dualist motifs are woven into Hindu scriptures such as the Upanishads and the Gita. The language of identity and that of difference are contained in the tradition; there is space for both mystical inwardness and outward devotion, for relationship to God and for identity with the Absolute.

Within the context of orthodox theology as seen in the Vedanta, the mainstream of Hindu interpretation of the sacred texts, probably the most genuine and important line of thinking lies uneasily between the two extremes. It is known as the Bhedābheda school, that is the 'identity and difference' school. Both Monism and Dualism, in other words, represent facets of sacred thought in the Hindu tradition. From one point of view *Brahman* is impersonal, one, and identical with the Self lying at the base of consciousness; from the other God is personal Creator and our Father and Mother. From one perspective, the One; from another the Lord of the many. Where this differs from Shankara's Monism is that the pluralism of the world, the personality of God, the duality of God and worshipper, and the gracious relationship of the Ultimate Self with the selves of living beings, are not unreal or secondary. They exist side by side with *Brahman* as Absolute and as Ineffable. The Divine Being has two sides, ineffable, unitary, ultimately One, on the one hand; and outward-looking, dynamic, ready to create and sustain the many, on the other hand. This two-aspect theory of God and the universe is a reflection of our own condition: we have two aspects, a consciousness and a body. It is reminiscent too of the notion that light under one aspect is waves and under another aspect, particles. It would probably be best to see the consciousness of Binode as expressed through the 'identity-and-difference' formula.

As an enlightened person he came to a realisation not only of his identity with the divine but also of his need to work in the world. He saw himself as an instrument of divine power, as well as being merged with the Absolute. At that full moon day, and indeed at subsequent repetitions of that auspicious date, he felt himself taken over by the divine power. At such a time, maybe, external magnetic conditions were more conducive to the enhancement of his sense of inner bliss and power. His consciousness, on that night in 1916, blossomed beyond the imageless contentment and insight of his Banaras absorption into a dynamic ecstasy of Identity-and-Difference. He felt God in action, and he felt oneness with God. Maybe he sensed the chants of devotion at the borders of his inner light.

At that time the pieces of his career 'came together'. From now on he was seen as a great teacher by those who followed him, and later known by the title Acharya. It has thus become customary to refer to him no longer as Binode or as the *brahmachari* but as the Acharya. In 1923 he also came to be known by a sacred name (much as monks and nuns in Christianity take a religious name, so is it in Hindu monastic movements). The name, Pranavananda, merits a brief word of explanation.

Many religious names in India end with Ananda, meaning 'bliss'. One of the three attributes of *Brahman*, together with consciousness and reality, is bliss – the ultimate bliss of the divine consciousness. So the bliss of the dedicated holy person reflects that of God. The other component in the name is *praṇava*, the title of the most sacred of all Sanskrit sounds, the mysterious syllable 'Om'. 'Om' sums up the essence of sound, and sound sums up the essence of Brahman. So in the Acharya's name is the name of names. It is worth noting how great an emphasis is placed in the orthodox Hindu tradition on the potency of sound. It is often thought that somehow the very sounds of the sacred language are primordial, and have existed for ever. The sound 'Om' is like an echo from before the creation of the world and is projected through the eons with which the cosmos is measured. It is like the Alpha and Omega of the Christian tradition. If there were anything like a translation of the Acharya's name it would be 'The bliss of Alpha and Omega'.

The night of his enlightenment experience was, then, a point of transition in the Acharya's consciousness. But the immediate effects were practical. In gathering round himself some trusted helpers, mostly youthful, the Acharya was developing a team who could be relied on to extend more systematically his concern for social improvement. He started humanitarian activities in the immediate region around Bajitpur. The hermitage was developed into a small ashram and most of the time the Acharya stayed there, occasionally going to eat at his parents' home. In the village he helped to develop cottage industries. The next few years were spent in such activities, and from this period we have a number of accounts of his social work. We shall come to some of these in a moment. But it is worth noting that the first impulse of Binode in this period was towards helping the poor and the sick. Only later did he develop the more ambitious organisations which helped to extend and expand his message. The period from 1916, the time of his illumination and the culmination of his period of *tapas* and self-training, until the foundation of his *Sangha* or monastic organisation, was an interim one, in which the emphasis was on building up local life. Later his attention was increasingly devoted to national problems.

Some of the scenes that have been recorded from this interim period are striking. In March 1918 a fisherman was catching fish at the mouth of the river in Bajitpur. He was far from his home in the Barishal district. As is the custom in those parts he was perched on a small, specially constructed platform above the waters. He suddenly contracted spasms of cholera, vomiting frequently and having violent diarrhoea. The fisherman had only one companion, his little boy, who ran and told Binode of the terrible illness. He came hurrying to the bank. There seemed to be too much difficulty involved in trying to remove the sick man from the platform, so Binode climbed onto it and nursed the sick man there. Alas, he died within a few hours, during the afternoon of that day.

The fisherman's ordeal was not over, for even in death he

45

needed dignity, and how was he, an untouchable, to be suitably cremated? No-one from the village was going to come and touch the polluting corpse of a stranger. Binode called some of his companions, including Nishi Datta, who has left us an account of the incident, and they gathered wood and twigs from abandoned bushes alongside the river and cremated the man. Next day the little boy was given some money and escorted home by one of the *ashram* workers.

For much of that period, into the following year of 1919, there was a severe cholera epidemic. Binode and his co-workers did what they could.

One of his disciples records a scene from April, 1918.

'. . . About eight o'clock in the morning I found myself in the *sadhana* cottage. In the outer apartment, on the same mat that is used by everybody; *Sadhuji* was resting, using his arm as a pillow. At his feet I noticed a piece of wet cloth. From this I guessed that he was too tired to spread it out after having bathed and changed, and that anyhow he had begun to rest. Not knowing anything about the situation I remained sitting. After a while he opened his eyes and asked me when I had arrived. Keeping his head on his left palm and his body-weight on this same elbow, he was in a half-reclining position.

Now he sat up and said: "In some parts of the village, cholera is spreading virulently. For the entire week, I have been nursing day and night, making arrangements for medicines and diet, and so on. There has been no breathing-space. I've just come from that end. What about your side?"

"No," I replied, "there is no cholera there."

He rejoined: "Everybody must be careful these days. Water must be boiled before you drink it. Take care of your food. No stale or hard-to-digest food should be taken. Moderation must be practised as an all-time rule. Carelessness in all these matters is the usual cause of this sort of illness. Burn incense and sulphur. Their smoke purifies polluted air. Camphor is good for diarrhoea, wrap some up in a piece of cloth and smell it now and then. Mind you, don't yield to fear. Fear will rob you of your power of resistance, and then disease will get the upper hand."

'Feeling tired, he went back to his half-reclining position and began nodding and sometimes his head would be about to touch the mat. After a while he lay and began snoring – a sure sign that he had gone into deep sleep. Really, I felt sorry for him and slightly guilty too for disturbing him in his rest at such an unusual and critical time. Mechanically and unconsciously the words came out of my lips "Let me go", a kind of habitual expression we used when we took leave of *Sadhuji*; and so I silently left the place.' (Swami Atmananda, *Sri Sri Yogachariya* 1st ed. p. 98.)

We see another glimpse of the social outreach of Binode's life during this period. On a bitterly cold night in January 1919, a Muslim villager came to Binode, led him out not too far from the village into a vast savannah which was used for grazing cattle and showed him a man lying there, to all appearances dead. But Binode put his finger under the man's nose; there was a light breath on it, so the fellow was not yet dead. He got the villager to run to his house and fetch a sheet of corrugated iron to serve as a stretcher. They carried the unconscious man to the ashram. There Binode lit a fire and heating up a rag over it started to rub the man to bring back a little warmth. Sure enough, after about two hours of this treatment there were signs of revival. Binode sent to his parents' house for some warm milk, which he fed to the patient. After the sun had risen and the chill was beginning to leave the air, the man opened his eyes and sat up. He rested there at the ashram until the middle of the day, and then had a proper meal. He was given two rupees and sent home. He was also a Muslim, like the villager who had shown him to the Acharya in the first place. Not surprisingly, rumours circulated that the Sadhu had restored the man to life – had, in other words, brought him back from the dead.

These, then, are some of the incidents surrounding the two or three years after 1916. Not only were Binode and his disciples active in combating cholera and other diseases endemic in the region, but they also did strenuous work during the devastating cyclone of 1919. They were involved in relief during the famine of 1921; Binode and his small band of self-denying youths travelled the villages of East Bengal, helping the starving, cremating and disposing of the dead, and giving advice on hygiene, diet and spiritual matters. Gradually his body of helpers grew to around five hundred, and his fame as a relief worker and socially committed holy man spread through Bengal. His work was about to be seen on a wider stage.

As for his sense of being an instrument of God, it is clear how it turned towards social effort and humanitarian goals. He and his followers were servants of the people, especially the poor and suffering, both Hindu and Muslim. His regard for Muslims is significant in view of the fact that he was also very firm on the need to have a self-reliant Hindu consciousness.

4
EARLY LIFE AT THE ASHRAM

The *ashram* was built, as we have seen, on a raised platform in what had been a dense piece of jungle that sometimes turned into a swamp after the monsoon. A canalised stream ran along one side of it. One reason why the area was cut off was that at first there was no bridge over the canal; in those early days Binode would wade across. There was a straw hut as the place for meditation and for the young *sadhu* to rest in. Another shed was for cooking. Later another tin building was put up as a place for assembly and the singing of *kirtans* or devotional hymns. One day the *sadhu* asked a disciple, Nishi Dutta, to fetch the family *brahmin*, Mahendra Chakravarty. That afternoon he arrived at the *ashram* and sat in the hut on a mat with Binode in front of him on a blanket. They negotiated about the land. This was attached to the Bana-Durga shrine, and was a religious endowment to Mahendra Chakravarty's family. It was now a question of transferring the land to the *ashram* legally. Probably the young holy man had already had permission from the *brahmin* to establish himself there. A deal was made and the land was sold to the *ashram* for 150 rupees. The *brahmin* had come to respect the young *sadhu*. Being versed in the scriptures he recognised, no doubt, that the attainment of yogic skills, austerity and deep meditation without help from anyone else had been a sure sign that the young man must have achieved high spiritual attainments in previous lives.

This is a recurrent theme of Hindu and other traditional Indian thinking; that boy (or girl) genius is a sign of a carry-over from the previous life. The fact that some children are mysteriously precocious, in music, learning, or in this case spirituality, is a sign that they have learned these things in a prior existence. So the remarkable and strange behaviour of Binode fitted into an intelligible world-view, and one which led the *brahmin* to treat his junior in this case with considerable respect. Thus in India sometimes the holy man rises above the most exalted of the priests.

After they had finished the transfer of the land, Mahendra Chakravarty said, '*Sadhu*, people say many things about you. Tell me with what strength, power and ability have you come and are working in the world?'

Binode is reported to have replied, in a matter of fact way, without any apparent pride (he was, as usual, unassuming in manner): 'After the Buddha, Shankara and Chaitanya, I have come down to work.'

Although meditation was a large part of the young *sadhu's* life, so also was devotion. As a centre for devotional practice the *ashram* became popular among the villagers and Binode's followers. We can get a feel for this through an account which has come down to us of a particular day and night in mid-February 1919. Binode sent for a certain Fedu Kaviraj, a poor man who was a skilled and enthusiastic hymn singer and had organised a choir. It was at the Durga Temple belonging to Kaviraj's family that Binode had had his vision of the divine Mother. Fedu sent messages all around warning them to be ready to go to the *ashram* that evening for a session of song and worship. Nishi Dutta on his way to tell Kaviraj, stopped off to buy about a kilo of sugar cakes. These hollow crispy cakes are a favourite in Bengal for hymn sessions. Since they are not much used apart from this they have come to be synonymous with *Hari Kirtan*, God-praising. He hurried back to prepare the lights – the oil lamp in the meditation place and a hurricane lamp in the shed for devotions. Another disciple, Suresh, got ready the drum and cymbals, and began himself to sing that famous hymn by Shankara which so frequently sums up the worship of Vishnu. It runs as follows:

50

'Day and night, morning and eve,
Winter and springtime come and leave,
Life goes by as time's moments skip.
But desire still holds us in its grip.
Worship Govinda, worship Govinda,
Worship Govinda: thought will not hinder
Death from arriving. Foolish thought,
Only in that is salvation sought.'

This Sanskrit hymn with its gentle refrain *'Bhaja Govinda, bhaja Govinda, bhaja Govinda'* was much prized by the Acharya and he recommended the hymn to all aspirants. He used to remark that it could awaken the sleeping man.

Govinda is a name for Krishna, literally meaning 'Cowkeeper' and refers to the God's youthful task of looking after the cattle around sacred Brindaban. The cows, like the girls whom he sported with, allegorically refer to human souls, whom Krishna loves as they love him. The hymn-singing is known in Bengal as *kirtan*, and often elsewhere as *bhajan*, a word whose root connects with *bhakti*, or loving devotion. This famous concept suggests more than worship of God; it implies participation in him, a kind of reciprocal inflowing of love, and an exchange of grace for devotion. The *kirtan* in its Bengali form was evolved by the saint Chaitanya (1485–1534), spiritual ancestor of today's Hare Krishnas. He emphasised the outpouring of God's grace and the need to worship him continuously and ecstatically. In philosophy his position was that of *bhedābheda*, but his whole emphasis was on the dualistic side of this doctrine.

Kaviraj and his singing party came at about 8 o'clock that evening. The *sadhu* entered the *kirtan*-shed and took his seat like the others on the ground. We can imagine the simple but enthusiastic scene. Kaviraj started off the songs, singing a verse and having the choir respond, mainly about Krishna's exploits in Brindaban: 'O Subal, tell me, O tell me, is this the same as my loving Brindaban?' More songs of this kind were sung, lauding Krishna and recalling his wonderful, tender

51

and merry exploits in the lovely region along the banks of the Jumna where he spent his young days.

The charm and spiritual attractiveness of the Krishna stories are important for us to understand, and are not always clearly perceived by Western readers. Like many other religious stories, the legends of Krishna existed on different levels. To escape the slaughter of children ordered by the evil king Kamsa, a Herod of North India, the baby Krishna was given to a cowherd, Nanda, and his wife Yasoda, to bring up, and so he spent his childhood and youth by the river Jumna in the area of Brindaban (or Vrndavana, literally 'herdforest') – now a famous centre of pilgrimage. Krishna as a boy was full of pranks: he would raid orchards like other naughty boys; he would play practical jokes on the *gopis* or milkmaids; and as he grew to young manhood he would make love to them. His favourite was Radha, who was transported by the delicious music of his flute and by his sultry blue charm. All this and much more in the vast body of stories about the God – for he was avatar or incarnation of the great Vishnu – was material for hymns and paintings, expressing and delineating the love of devotees for the beautiful holiness and personality of the Divine Being. It was this cluster of tales that inspired the singers that night when they started the joyful worship in the shed at Binode's *ashram*.

After a while the *sadhu* expressed the wish that they might sing about the saint Chaitanya's monastic life. Kaviraj obliged by beginning the lines:

> 'O. Nimai, O my darling,
> Where did you go, leaving your poor mother?'

The song echoed the sad weeping of the saint's mother when he left her to pursue the religious life.

The singing went on till about one o'clock in the morning, when as is traditional in Bengal the puffy sugar cakes were scattered among the worshippers. Then other sweet cakes were distributed and the night's celebrations came to a calm and cheerful end. *Sadhu* Binode took some sweets and retired to bed.

This charming portrayal of the devotional life of Binode's *ashram* reflects the way in which in much of India Bhakti religion also provides for a warm, congregational mode of expressing community spirit. It enables ordinary people as well as those more particularly pledged to the religious life to gather together in order to sing the praises of the one God.

The *ashram* became more popular as time went on and consequently it was thought necessary to build a bridge over the canal which separated the village from the *ashram*. *Sadhu* Binode thought it best to use a tall tree as the main part of the bridge with bamboo as scaffolding or hand-rails. He therefore went to see Majumdar, the *zamindar* (main landowner) of the village, who happened to be sympathetic to the good works of the *sadhu*. When they arrived they discovered that Majumdar was very much preoccupied. They asked him what the matter was. He explained that as a householder he was plagued with troubles and that in particular he was uncertain about some law cases in the court which were giving him considerable anxiety.

Binode paused for a while and then said with a smile: 'Is that all? Let peace be with you. The verdict of the court is in your favour!'

Overwhelmed with astonishment Majumdar exclaimed: 'Are you sure, *Sadhuji*?'

'I am sure,' answered Binode.

A few days later the news of the landowner's victory in the litigation reached him from the town. This incident reinforced Majumdar's respect for the young saint. However, the tall tree which Binode had come to ask permission to cut down was not used in the end, for when the young man gazed at the huge, lively, productive berry tree, he felt that it was painful to cut it down and a great waste. As it turned out, however, they discovered another suitable tree which they used to build the bridge across the canal as they had planned.

In 1919 Binode was greatly saddened by the death of his younger brother, Bholā. He said of the bereavement: 'My right-hand broke'. Bholā would accompany his saintly brother during periods of meditation: when Binode went out to meditate in the cremation ground at night, to the wide savannah near the river, or to sit under the tree by the shrine to Durga, his brother would stand silently nearby to ward off any beast or human being who might either disturb the meditating saint or be frightened by the sight of the still, contemplative figure looming out of the Bengali night. If anything, his brother was stronger than Binode and showed his capacity for endurance in these long vigils. As he lay dying, Binode initiated him, and so Bholā became his first initiated disciple. He uttered a sacred formula or *mantra* as the young man was passing away and perhaps these were the last words that Bholā heard in this life.

It should be explained that a common feature of Hindu ordination, when a *guru* takes a disciple, or when someone enters into a new holy state, is the use of a *mantra* which is often individually selected for the person being ordained by the spiritual preceptor. The *mantra* symbolises the way in which sacred knowledge and insight is handed down from teacher to disciple, and it reflects too the common Hindu view of the intrinsic power of words themselves to effect changes in those who hear them. Thus at the solemn moment when a disciple is brought into the inner circle of the teacher the words reverberate cosmically and psychologically to transform the life of the initiate. The young Bholā, dying so soon, perhaps thought that his older brother with all his saintly power could save him from death; but Binode commented sadly 'It cannot happen without the special plan or will of the All-Dispenser'. And so it was that now Binode sat alone by night, traversing the paths of his divinely illuminated conscious, with no devoted shadow close by to defend him from the perils of the outside world.

Although Binode was no longer living at home, he would from time to time delight his mother and the other members of his family by going to the house and accepting a simple meal from the hands of his relatives, as they sat in the shed outside the house which contained the area for husking rice and for cooking. He would often be accompanied by one of his close companions. His mother would look at him with amazement, trying to understand the destiny of her son, who was now more widely recognised as a holy man of increasing power and influence. She would say to him importunately, 'What is the harm of coming home? I crave to see you.' The *sadhu* would give no reply, but simply smile benignly and sweetly at his mother.

His activities extended to helping the villagers in their economic plight. He had the idea that it would be useful to help generate some cottage industry. Once in the middle of March in 1920 he returned from a trip to Calcutta and called at his parents' home. He was immediately surrounded by his brothers' wives and by the other women. When one of the men of the extended family entered, the *sadhu* said to him that he would like to take one of the large trees in the old homestead land. He offered to pay if any of the men in the family should object. But the family gave him the tree and he went to the piece of land where the trees grew, and selected an appropriate specimen. Later on he received other trees from other families. In all he got permission to cut down five trees. After lunch that day, the *sadhu* and his companion Nishi Dutta went to see what progress the labourer who had been told to cut down the trees had made. On the way they engaged two carpenters. That evening Binode revealed to some of the villagers, including Muslims, his plan for a new industry. The trees meanwhile were brought to the *ashram* and chopped up by the labourer. The following day Binode went to a nearby town, brought back another huge tree with him in a boat and declared that he now had the wood to make three hundred or more spinning wheels. This was a prelude to a few days of enthusiastic activity when Binode supervised the making not only of spinning wheels, but also of rice pedals (small machines for husking rice) and handlooms. These were distributed in Bajitpur and neighbouring villages. As regards the husking of rice, there was a problem about where to instal the machines. The *sadhu* suggested his own family compound. But there were objections to the idea of women of different castes coming there to work, and eventually another site was chosen.

Binode himself, we can see here, was indifferent to questions of caste. But always it remains a persistent factor in Indian village life. Its power has many dimensions. It establishes a whole confederation of freemasonries, groups of mutual support bound together both by ritual and overlapping patterns of consanguinity. But its power has also a dimension which is more difficult to convey to those who do not belong to Indian society. This is the dimension of purity and impurity. The fabric of caste is interwoven with various tabus on what is impure and what measures can be taken to purify and to avoid impurities. The left hand, menstruation, inadvertent ritual mistakes, killing, certain forms of travel – a whole crowd of actions can bring impurity. Such contaminations have to be dealt with by rituals of purification. But in addition certain people, being low caste or untouchable, can bring contamination by their close presence. This is a powerful reinforcement of the caste structure: spiritual and physical contamination is a strong disincentive to haphazard mingling with the wrong sort of person. Perhaps Westerners can understand something of this feeling if they ever edge further off a pavement in order to avoid coming too close to a beggar or tramp. Caste is glued together by a system of mutual avoidance. Binode was against divisions within Hinduism, yet like other such leaders he could not escape the grip of the system even in his own family.

His concern for generating village industry in the neighbourhood was a sign of his wider social programme, still forming in his mind. Already in 1919 a devastating cyclone had drawn him into emergency aid for the stricken, and his desire to blend religion and action attracted to him an increasing number of young people, who at first became his disciples informally and later were more formally enrolled in the organisations he instituted, culminating in his creation of the Sangha. He provided inspiration which mobilised the idealism of the young and he remained close to the nationalist struggle throughout his life.

A typical incident, recorded by Nishi Datta, occurred during the days when Binode was organising the making of the spinning wheels for the villagers. At two in the morning there came a soft knock on the door of the *ashram* where Binode and Nishi Datta lay asleep. A voice gently and urgently said: 'Are you there?'

Who could it be, thought Datta, at this hour? The voice repeated the question more urgently. The *sadhu* knew who they were, and told Datta to open the door, though on no account to light the lamp. Binode, as we have already seen, was known to have some sympathy for the secret societies who plotted violent revolution against the British, even if he did not share their methods. He admired their dedication, toughness and patriotism. Who was he therefore to turn them away in their hour of need? In case the police were watching, he did not want the lamp lit. Nishi Datta hurried off to get some rice and lentils. This simple meal he cooked up in no time at all. The young men, seven in all, had not eaten all day. They were famished and exhausted. They wolfed down the meal. The *sadhu* served them water in the dark, out of a small jug, urging them to take their time. They were in haste to get away again. The *sadhu* apologised for the poverty of the meal (it was of course the sort of basic food on which he himself subsisted).

'There were only rice and lentils: could these fill you properly?' he said.

They replied that such gratifying food is rare, even on a feast day. Hunger is the best sauce and terror the stimulant of gratitude. Fearfully, they got up and went out into the dark night, making their way across the eastern savannah flanking Bajitpur.

These were turbulent times in India. The war – the Great War, as the British began to call it – had raised hopes in India, for Indian troops had fought on the Western Front and in the Middle East. Surely India was to be rewarded with a better status? Would she not deserve that self-determination which was the guiding principle of the Versailles Treaty, now being forged in France? 1919 not only

57

saw Versailles and the zenith of President Wilson's hopes for a better world; it also saw the terrible Amritsar massacre, when General Dyer shot down demonstrators in so manic a fashion (and in the following year was rewarded with a hero's accolade back in Britain). It was also the beginning of Gandhi's major campaign for control of the Congress. Nationalism, both violent and constitutional, was rife in Bengal: and what Bengal thinks today, it was said, India thinks tomorrow. Even in remote Bajitpur the waves of these events were to ripple around, disturbing the placid surface of rural life.

Certain ideas were forming in Binode's mind as he immersed himself in social work and relief activities and led the enthusiastic young on missions of mercy and help. In the long reaches of the night, while he meditated at the charnel ground, and as he dropped to sleep after days filled with hectic activity, he brought together different feelings, visions and dreams that spurred him towards the organisation which was to embody the principles implicit in his divine mission.

One strand in these feelings, of course, was his realisation that there had been some higher descent into his own consciousness, that he had been 'taken over', as we might say, by God. His destiny was shining, but it had to lead naturally out of his birth in this muddy green land of East Bengal over which the spirit of the Buddha and many other saintly and divine figures presided.

Another strand was the awareness that he had the charismatic power to attract the young. Could not some of these eager souls be channelled through discipline to become a mighty source of service to Mother India and to suffering humanity? Already he was beginning the rudiments of what was later to blossom into his Sangha. Here at his hermitage there were planted the seeds of a much more luxuriant growth. And his own preoccupation with the state of *brahmacharya*, which helped to give him the power, charisma and energy to carry on his holy and dedicated life, could be spread to these other young people. They too could be dedicated in continence to the life of service.

A third strand in his thinking was his concern for India. In

58

particular he wished to reinvigorate the Hindu community. As we have seen he related well to Muslims and often helped them. But his heart lay with the Hindu community. They had been enfeebled and humiliated by a double conquest. On the one hand they had fallen under the yoke of the Mughals. Even the holy city of Banaras bore the imprint of Islamic rule; Aurangzeb's tall mosque dominated the skyline above the myriad temples which huddled along the *ghats*. On the other hand India was now under alien British governance and the sacred religion was often attacked by Christian missionaries and arrogant administrators. No wonder Hindus often displayed unwelcome sycophancy and a servile lack of spirit. Binode ruminated that a certain manly vigour was needed to combat this weakness; the Hindu must hold up his head. In this he was sympathetic to those tough, wild young men who fondled pistols by night and dreamed of bombs and shattering British pomp. Although he did not use or approve of their methods, he liked their guts – more, indeed, than he liked the non-violence of Mahatma Gandhi's spreading message. He saw himself as an alternative to the Gujarati lawyer.

A fourth strand was his drive towards social and humanitarian service. His work in the cyclone and later in famine conditions came to be well recognised. He was conscious that he must go beyond the example of other wise and holy persons in the Bengali tradition – such as his own *guru* in Gorakhpur, and even the saintly Ramakrishna – and involve himself directly in worldly activity. This action was to be directed towards raising consciousness among the peasants of his native land, and beyond in wider India. Could all these ideas be welded together? We shall look in the next chapter at the shape of his Sangha and the ideas behind it.

Meanwhile, in the four or five years after his enlightenment experience, he was laying some of the foundations. He had found his destiny: it was neither to be that of his fellow students who went on higher in education and the professions; nor was it to be that of those who bravely went underground in patriotic terrorism. His path lay in between,

59

and he felt it was traced for him by the Divine Being whose near presence in his own soul was the dominating factor in his conscious life.

His desire for national reinvigoration was reinforced from two directions. One influence was the fact that Hindus in East Bengal were a minority, and in the shifting tides of political change might need to stand up for themselves. The other involved a more directly religious observation: Binode had already noticed corruption and oppression in the national Hindu holy places of pilgrimage. We shall see that both these causes were to attract his attention and stimulate his practical policies of help and reform.

Meanwhile we may best symbolise the early life of the *ashram* by the story of the great 1919 cyclone. The onset of the storm was ominous. From Dacca to Faridpur the sky darkened. Over Bajitpur as elsewhere the clouds raced swollen across the howling sky, disgorging torrents which blew almost horizontal, whipping, drenching, tormenting trees, cattle and all living things, churning and puckering the canal outside the *ashram*. There the Acharya and some of his disciples were gathered in the worship shed, singing songs of adoration to God, as was often their custom. But the battering noise on the corrugated roof was frightening, and the structures threatened to take off into the wet rush of the mighty winds. The whole day passed in this terrible manner. At last Binode and the other young men decided to make a run for it and scurried pell-mell to his family house, which was brick built and more secure. Once there he could imagine what might be happening to those less protected. He decided to go out into the storm alone (for he did not wish to risk his workers' lives) and help others to come to the house for refuge. His mother held his hand, trying to keep him there. She clung to his hand in terrible fear. It was not long since Bholā's death. Could she bear to risk another son? But he persuaded her to let him go, and in the gathering dusk struggled to the village. Trees were snapping like matches, roofs were being blown away, walls crumbled, the streams were swollen, and the wind made it hard even to stand up.

Amid the chaos he gathered some fifty people back to his parents' home. In one house, as he was bringing an old person out, the roof blew off. In another he had to hold up the thatched palm-leaf roof while the family crawled out from under. But life and death, he reflected, flow from *karma* and the merciful will of God. After two hours of work, his home began to look like a refugee camp.

He then went to the Muslim quarter, where many of the poor were waiting to die, in the name of Allah, accepting his will. He gathered twenty-five or thirty of the worst sufferers and took them to the house of the *zamindar*, who could hardly refuse the *brahmachari's* plea that he should shelter his unfortunate tenants. Binode seemed like an angel of mercy, appearing there before his door in the screaming storm. Binode then went to the low caste area: scarcely a house in the tumbledown quarter had not been ripped apart by the cyclone. It was about 1 o'clock in the morning when he reached the people there. He escorted them to a nearby family home built of brick. Then he struggled on, having regretted that he could not supply dry clothes to the sodden refugees. He went to the village of the untouchables, poor cobblers and leather-workers, and escorted them too to relative safety. Everyone is equal: there is no untouchability – such was his conviction. By 6 in the morning he was back at his parents' house where he had left about fifty people.

He went out early as the storm subsided to beg for rice from the better off. He had a small supply from his own, earlier alms begging. By the afternoon he and his young men were able to organise the beginnings of relief work. In two or three days they had a regular community kitchen to feed the hungry, and a fund was started to provide clothes and shelter. There was also Government help. Meanwhile the rivers had risen, and in the swollen torrents many people and animals were swept off. The disaster was on a terrible and daunting scale.

The *ashram* was not too badly affected. The cottage was leaning, and fencing had been swept away. But Binode and his followers were able to establish it as a centre for coordinating aid. Students from nearby villages were able to come to the *ashram* by boat to meet him. He gave them money where necessary and instructed them in relief methods. He told them how to collect rice and money and how they should in due course build up a permanent stock of food and materials against some future disaster. He stressed the need for good organisation. Good will was wonderful but by itself it was not enough. And so in the days and weeks after the cyclone the *ashram* was the hub of an expanding circle of service. Poor people were fed. Volunteers helped to rebuild houses. The dead were cremated or buried.

In the wake of the cyclone he set up two social service centres near Bajitpur, the Madaripur Sevashrama and Khuln Sevashrama. Here was a foretaste of his later establishment of the Sangha, to which we shall come in the next chapter. According to an eye-witness account the Acharya delivered an address on the day after the cyclone. Perhaps it has been somewhat more formally recorded than his actual words at the time were expressed, but it gives a good idea of the sentiments which he held and which animated the eager young men whom he inspired to work for the needy in this time of disaster.

'Such a terrific cyclone has never visited this part of the world. Even the old people never witnessed one such as this. Marsh lands and lands by the river are worst hit. The fishermen who were out fishing in marshy areas are nearly all dead. The lower middle class people have suffered most. This cyclone has added further difficulty to those who are already in distress. Oh, they will not survive if nothing is done for them. At this perilous moment everyone should try and do something. If man does not feel for man, where is his manliness? Even animals help one another in common danger. If man is not up to the standard he is worse than an animal. It is through service to the needy that man can forget himself, his narrow-mindedness and selfishness will disappear and he will become liberal in spirit. He will feel strong like a lion. His reasoning power will be free from impotency. He will become great.

It is selfishness which breaks his backbone. He becomes weak and useless. Unconcerned about others' needs, man is busy only with himself and it is then that jealousy shows its ugly head. In his guilty conscience he will have no courage to inspire others in selfless service. Anyway, do as much as you can in this situation. From the *ashram* relief is being sent out. Let me know if you need anything as far as relief is concerned.'

One can imagine the young men, slender in white slacks or *dhotis*, their eyes glowing, idealistic middle-class and poorer students, ready to follow the directions of this burly young holy man, himself only in his early 20s; and Binode sitting by his sodden, leaning hut, in the steamy sun after the great rains, noting down details of the extent of the villages' needs as the students from the area round about recounted the statistics of misfortune. Already his reputation was spreading. Soon his *ashram* would acquire a more than local significance.

5
THE CREATION OF
THE SANGHA

As the events of the 1919 cyclone showed, Binode was moving towards the creation of a formal organisation to express and channel his ideals of service and celibacy. Already the group of young people around him had among them those who wished to give up the world in order to follow the ideals of *brahmacharya* and national uplift. He was already encouraging his followers to be systematic in the collection and administration of money and supplies. But it seems that he preferred a step-by-step establishment of the Sangha or Order. First he had built the *ashram* itself. Then he had brought about the start of service *ashrams* at Madaripur and Khulna. Later he was to initiate *brahmacharins* as his disciples. Finally in 1923 and 1924 he consolidated the idea of the Sangha.

In 1921 a severe famine in Bengal occupied the Acharya and his followers for most of the year. Khulna, Satkshira and Sundarban were the worst affected areas. Sundarban was particularly wild, with swamps noted for their dangerous snakes and forests in which the dread and beautiful Bengal tiger roams. Often it was necessary to wade through swamps and streams to get to the starving villagers, but Acharya Binode knew little fear in these exhausting journeys. He and his band of helpers – which now expanded to more than five hundred young people – were reported by the newspapers in glowing terms. A well-known scientist, Sir P. C. Roy, had organised in Calcutta a Central Relief Committee which worked with the Acharya and his men, and another fundraising committee in Bombay. He wrote: 'Hundreds of workers he recruited in no time. Would this relief work have been possible only with the money, rice and clothes that were collected? . . . It is the management of a competent leader that made the thing successful.'

The priority, as the Acharya saw it, was to replace lost cattle, especially the bullocks that were essential for ploughing. He brought in animals from other parts of India and supplies of seed-rice to enable the peasants to make a new start.

The effect of these strenuous activities was to create a pool of young people who served in such relief work and who might have some inclination towards a more permanent life of dedication to humanity. The Acharya kept his eye on the most promising of these youths, and the mutual chemistry between teacher and aspirant led to the events of the Maghipurnima Day of 1922. To that we shall come in a moment. Meanwhile the immediate famine relief was over, but there was quite a lot of money left in the fund – about 60,000 rupees. Binode suggested to Sir P. C. Roy and others that constructive work to create new cottage industries should be undertaken. His earlier experience at Bajitpur came into play. It was decided to start the spinning and weaving of cloth and mats in a number of centres (Asasuni, Mitratentulia, Buddhata and Pratapnagar). After some months workers also went to Comilla, a far-off district, to learn how to grow and work with cane and bamboo. The idea was that even if the crop should fail, the poor people had something to tide them over. It was a way of helping rural reconstruction. One who was there at this time recalls: 'Still fresh in my memory is the picture of the reviving of the dying villages: thousands of spinning wheels revolving; handlooms day and night making noise in weaving cloth; cane and bamboo baskets being stored in bulk; new free schools introducing a different sort of curriculum; libraries getting new kinds of books; charitable dispensaries treating not only men but animals as well; the workers constantly going round the whole area to supervise these activities; bells echoing three times a day from *ashram* temples during prayer. Everyone in the area is loudly praising (the) *brahmachari*.' Thus wrote Swami Advaitananda, one of his early disciples.

After the relief work and its follow-up many of the students went back home but some stayed on and prepared to make the trip to Bajitpur. The occasion was the holy day (for it had become such) when the enlightenment of Binode was remembered and celebrated back at the mother *ashram*. There the aspirants encountered a different leader from the man they had followed in the field of relief. Here at home he was fully in authority, moving and talking as if in total control both of himself and his milieu.

But despite his charismatic power he did not at this time accept his followers as *chelas* or full disciples. He was to wait six years from the time of his illumination before any such relationship was established. In this he differed from some modern gurus with whom the West has become familiar. Only slowly did he come to institute discipleship, either because he did not yet feel he had a command from Above or because he perceived that his followers were not ready.

The life of the *ashram* was enhanced on this day of the year, as on other occasions, with chanting and singing the praises of Krishna. The atmosphere was charged with intense piety. The young initiates went through the regular rituals necessary to their forthcoming status: they had their heads shaved and fasted a whole day and night, performing together the rites of *upanayana homa* which in traditional India signals the transition into the state of *brahmacharya*, when a young person is invested with the sacred thread and embarks on the life of the *brahmacharin*. The ceremony reached its climax when the initiates dressed in white loincloths and white *chadars* (wrappings for the upper part of the body) awarded to them by Binode himself, and were given too the *mantram* or sacred initiatory formula pledging them to renunciation and sacrifice. They repeated the following vow:

'I will never shake off from my heart the most sacred *Mantram* of renunciation and sacrifice;
Never shall I leave aside this holy attire of a recluse nor shall I ever attempt to violate any rules of the *Sannyasa-Ashrama* until I realise the Self;
Never shall I be a dupe to sensuality;

I shall devote myself always to the realisation of the One
and the Immutable through unflinching adherence to
Truth;
I will live a life of celibacy.'

This was the formal beginning of what was later to be the
Sangha. The young people were fired with the thought of a
career of self-sacrifice, and for a while the Acharya was
greatly exercised with the task of instructing them. He was
also busy with continued work of reconstruction and relief;
he spent much time in Calcutta, still the commercially dominant city of India, meeting prominent men who might give
him support and walking the streets begging for money for
his fund to help the destitute. He now had four *ashrams* to
supervise, including the mother *ashram* at Bajitpur.

He left the young disciples free to pursue their varied
interests. These tended to develop in three different directions. One was towards rural relief, and the important work of
setting up in other villages some of the cottage industries
which had already been pioneered at Bajitpur. Another
direction was the revival of older patterns of education –
drawing upon the Hindu tradition to establish country
colleges where instruction would cover not just intellectual
and physical development but spiritual and moral growth as
well. This involved an implicit criticism of the Western-style
education which the young men themselves had experienced.
Indeed these directions which they explored expressed a
populism not unlike that found among the Russian intelligentsia of a generation or two earlier. The followers of the
Acharya were Bengali populists, looking to a revival of ancient
values and prizing the life of the villagers who were the essence
of India, both now and in times gone by. As the young men
taught the poor to become more self-sufficient through
spinning, weaving, making baskets and chairs, and restocking
and improving their plots of land, they saw in the faces of the
villagers a grateful reminder of India's primordial strengths.

The third direction which some of them took was towards
the life of the spirit: the meditation, prayer and fasting which

67

were the ancient practices of the *sannyasins*. They considered that if there were not those among them who pursued this strictly spiritual path, the movement could easily weaken and lose its transcendental outreach. After all they were following the ideal of *sannyasa*.

In so far as the Acharya thought of his followers as *sannyasins* he was of course reflecting an ancient ideal, but in a new form. The old doctrine of the four stages of life or *ashramas* (the same word incidentally as for a hermitage or spiritual centre) implied that one begins as a *brahmacharin*, continues as a householder raising a family, then begins to leave the home and family, perhaps living in a hut in a nearby forest, and finally becomes a genuinely homeless, holy man totally dedicated to the spiritual quest. But here the group followed a fusing of first and last stages: the students were also *sannyasins*. In this they adhered to the forms of Hindu monasticism, influenced in part by the Sangha ideal of the Buddhists. In addition, most of the *brahmacharins* of Binode saw their destiny as involving work in the world. It is true that the young people of the third direction could take advantage of a retreat house that came to be built up near Gaya. But the movement as a whole had grown out of social service in the villages, and it was there, in the world of the suffering poor and of a renascent Hindu identity, that their major tasks were to be performed. What then was the meaning of their ideal of renunciation? It can be explained somewhat as follows.

The white robe of the *brahmacharin* was a sign of renunciation, but that renunciation had its positive pole – a sense of the Transcendent. Like other *sannyasins* these young men were a perpetual reminder in their own persons of the Other Shore, of God's heaven. The Acharya as their leader was a bridge between this and the other world. But they saw God's grace and power as transforming this world. So the movement was amphibious, swimming in this world but often walking on the solid ground of the other world for replenishment and new energy. It was reasonable, then, that near Gaya there should be a centre for meditation and retreat. The location too was an echo of Buddhism, for Gaya was the place of the Buddha's Enlightenment and in some ways Binode saw his own calling as analogous to that of India's greatest, ancient, spiritual teacher.

If 1922 was a tiring year, with all the activities of the new organisation being developed and the need to raise money ever pressing, the new year of 1923 was soon graced by the next stage of the movement's growth. It was again on the auspicious Maghipurnima day in February, commemorating the leader's enlightenment experience of seven years before, that it was decided to adopt the name by which the organisation of Binode's followers became known. The name was the Bharat Sevashram Sangha. Each component of the name is significant and expresses the movement's worldview.

First of all, the word *Bharat* signifies India. The ancient name of Bharata was given to the Indo-Gangetic plain, the heartlands of the Aryans and scene of most of the action of the Great Epic Mahābhārata. Later the term came to be used of the whole of India. So Binode saw his task essentially in Indian terms. It is true that later the Sangha was to establish Indian cultural centres abroad. But the heart of the mission was to be India itself. Lying behind this is the idea that the Vedic tradition is the highest expression of spiritual truth – India's offering to the whole world. And although Binode, as we have noted, was solicitous of his Muslim neighbours and the Muslim poor, he was convinced of the superior spirituality of the Indian (both Hindu and Buddhist) tradition. He was keen to serve the Hindu world and to revive it. He was thus a Hindu patriot in spirit.

The term *Seva* refers to service. The organisation was to be a service-oriented one. It was to be practical and efficacious, not just spiritual; and it was above all a movement aimed towards the service of the people of India. So although he did not deny that there was need of seclusion and self-control, he considered that ultimately such a desire for living alone in the hermitage should be realised only metaphorically. The stable, peaceful mind is the best cave. And so one can have inner stability and serenity while going out to perform services for the world.

The term *ashrama* in the title refers to the four stages of life but in the present context more particularly to the ideals lying behind them, of renunciation, self-control, truth and continence.

Finally, *Sangha* has powerful echoes of Buddhism: it means 'organised community'. Binode followed in the footsteps of the Buddha, as he saw them. But he also thought of this new group – focused, compact, well-organised – as being a way of bringing cohesion to the aspirations and life of the masses, disintegrated and depressed as they were by poverty, conquest and the decay of ancient ideals. It was appropriate that Binode should look back to Buddhism which had survived longer in Bengal than in most other parts of India.

It should be noted that at the time of the naming of the organisation, the Acharya was emphatic that the Sangha should not be named after an individual, because no matter how important an individual might be he could never be higher than a nation which incorporated its accumulated *tapasya* and inspired experiences from the very dawn of history. So the Sangha was named after India as the historical repository of the divine ideals which the movement sought to promote and express.

Later in the same year Binode formally took the name Acharya Pranavananda, and we can think of 1923–1924 as the crucial period when his movement solidified and made the transition from being a largely *ad hoc* relief organisation to an Order whose influence stretched across Bengal and beyond.

The movement proved to be a kind of extension of the Acharya's own personality. He was the President and no elections were held, although not unnaturally after his death the more conventional structures of a religious society came into being. But under Swami Pranavananda's guidance it quickly spread and it gained a fine reputation for good works. Among those who much later were to pay tribute to it were Jawaharlal Nehru and Indira Gandhi. The former wrote, in August 1957:

'I well remember my visit to Anjar in Kutch soon after the earthquake demolished that village. I was much impressed by the good work done by various organisations and especi-

70

ally by the Bharat Sevashram Sangha. I expressed my appreciation of it there and I am repeating it now.'

Mrs Gandhi wrote in May 1970:

'All the great figures of our national life have taught us that service is the highest form of culture and religion. The Bharat Sevashram Sangha has served the people with devotion in times of difficulty. My good wishes for the branch of the Sangha which is being established at Srinivaspuri in the capital.' (These quotations are from the annual report of the Bharat Sevashram Sangha.)

These were tributes from much later but they reflect the respect which the humanitarian work of the movement attracted from the beginning. Other aspects of the Acharya's organisation were, as we shall see in due course, controversial: but not the dedication of the young *sannyasins* and *brahmacharins* of the Order.

The aims of the Sangha were as follows: first, to help the distressed, to nurse the sick, to feed the hungry and to clothe the naked; second, to organise relief in times of disaster; third, to establish free educational and medical institutions and charitable societies; fourth, to improve the social and material conditions of the people by encouraging home industries; fifth, to promote educational facilities especially for outcaste and depressed communities; sixth, to propagate and foster the spiritual and cultural heritage of India; seventh, to promote better understanding and unity with the followers of different faiths; and eighth, to create an atmosphere conducive to moral and spiritual growth in India.

It is notable that there is a special emphasis on the poor and the untouchables. The Acharya considered that part of the problem of Hindu independence was brought about by the social divisions within the people. Greater equality was a precondition of national liberation.

The increase in the work of the Sangha was symbolised by the expansion of its accommodation in Calcutta. It was in a

71

hired thatch hut in 1922, moved from there to a flat and thence to a big hall. The Sangha had also to maintain its four *ashrams*, a couple of centres for training young followers and various schools and dispensaries. The need for money led to the devising of the system of preaching parties of a dozen or more young people under the guidance of a more senior monk. These groups would go from door to door in villages and towns, and could undertake various tasks. They could preach and conduct propaganda for the movement. They could support one another. Single preachers were exposed to temptations and pressures. Already the Sangha had met opposition, for instance, from followers of Mahatma Gandhi. Their talk of restoring the glories of the Vedic Age seemed old-fashioned to the Gandhians. Moreover politicians from the educated élite had quite different ideals from those of the Acharya's *sannyasins*. So mutual support in a preaching party was useful in the face of such scepticism and the temptations of the world. The preaching party was a kind of mobile monastery and could conduct its own meditation sessions, worship and scriptural readings. Moreover the size of the group had organisational advantages. It was big enough to mobilise quickly to organise a large religious demonstration. The party structure also helped when aid was suddenly needed in one part of the country or another. Finally, the system allowed the maintaining of contact with the masses. All these aspects of the group organisation also made it easier to provide a flow of funds for continuing the varied activities of the Sangha.

The amount of relief work performed over the years makes formidable reading. Members of the Sangha were to take part in the alleviation of distress in major floods in Bengal, Assam, Bihar, Uttar Pradesh, Rajasthan, Madhya Pradesh, Gujarat and Tamil Nadu. They were at work in the famines of East Bengal, Gujarat and Bihar. In the terrible wartime famine of 1942–3 they maintained nine kitchens for giving out free food in Bengal. In the half century from 1921 they were at work in many of the fifty cyclones which struck Eastern India from the Himalayas to the Orissa coast.

Sangha workers nursed the sick and brought succour in the cholera epidemics of 1927 in Orissa, in 1928 in Banaras and in other outbreaks in 1929, 1951, 1956 and in 1960 (the last in East Pakistan, now Bangladesh). It is estimated that they helped to save up to ten thousand people in these cholera outbreaks. They also gave relief to victims of earthquakes, fires and communal riots. Even at this level alone the Sangha was a potent force both during the Acharya's lifetime and after his death. Also important (we shall deal with the topic later) was the help given to pilgrims at the major sacred centres of North India.

Although the original aims of the Sangha were as listed above, in 1927 a Memorandum of Association was procured to put the organisation on a legal basis, and the aims were then somewhat expanded, partly to include the matter of pilgrimage. Thus they were listed as: spiritual and cultural propaganda and reform; the spread of education on the basis of spiritual and moral principles; the purification of holy places and the restoration of their primitive spiritual atmosphere; social reformatory and organisational activities; and the spread of Indian culture in foreign lands. At the same time a Board of Trustees was set up with the Acharya as President and Treasurer.

The rules which he laid down for the Sangha were strict. Members of the Brotherhood should never live, travel or work alone, nor should they mix with householders or their families except for the purpose of getting alms and contributions. Thus they should not accept invitations to eat alone in any house. They should not criticise the ideals or activities of the Sangha and should rigorously obey all communally decided directives. They should not harbour illwill or any hostile feelings, nor should they sow any dissension within the Order; and individual aspirations or ideals, however noble, should be sacrificed before the decisions of the Sangha.

The whole emphasis was upon the Sangha as an extension of the life of the Acharya, and likewise as a spiritual journey, embarked on in a community, towards the Eternal. The

73

individual members would be merged in a wider whole. There are some parallels with the Christian Church seen as the body of Christ. The Sangha was the body of the Acharya.

This parallel might strike some readers as startling. But it should be remembered that the followers of the Acharya (and the Acharya himself) perceived him as indeed divine, as having been taken over by the Almighty, and as a kind of conduit of the Absolute. This was increasingly expressed in a ritual way in the life of the movement and culminated in ceremonies performed in major pilgrimage centres, and inaugurated at the home *ashram* in 1924. The Acharya began to receive honours due to God.

It began in March 1924, or a little earlier. One of his disciples, Swami Vedananda, went to celebrate a festival at Asasuani. He suggested to some of the others that they might perform some ceremony to signify a new attitude of *bhakti* towards their leader but the others were preoccupied with more practical and to them, at that time, more important tasks. The disciple decided to go ahead by himself. It was a time during the full moon of March when there was a major festival, and people thronged the *ashram*. There was singing, assemblage of devotees and devotional discourses. Food and sweetmeats were served to the faithful; but the chanting, joy, enthusiasm, flowers, incense, delicacies made no impression on the disciple: until he decided to enter the Acharya's hut. There he took flowers and *bel* leaves and offered these oblations at his feet.

The Acharya kindly and affectionately said: 'Now go and take some food.'

This was the first instance, so far as is known, when the Acharya allowed himself to be venerated thus; and it is significant that eight years had elapsed between the time of his illumination and this moment.

In November of the same year the same disciple had a series of visions. Whenever he closed his eyes in meditation he found he was seeing the Acharya sitting on a beautiful throne within a circle of stupendous light. This formidable and overwhelming vision stunned the young man. He and another disciple decided on the morning after the full moon day to worship the Acharya, seating him on the altar of the *ashram* temple in Madaripur and attending him with all the relevant rituals. From this period onwards the Acharya expected his followers to act in this way and to treat him as a divine *guru* and not just as leader of a movement. After three days or so there was a similar ceremony at the Khulna Ashram; and gradually such *gurupuja* or guru-worship became more public, culminating in ceremonies at Banaras and elsewhere, during which he would float on a ceremonial barge down the sacred river, on a high throne in orange robe, a splendid, strong figure with some of the accoutrements of God, such as the trident.

The trident was the symbol above all of Shiva. It reflected the three qualities or *guṇas* which, blended together, formed Nature and reflected the three functions of God as Creator, Preserver and Destroyer. For in Indian thinking, with clear logic, not only is God the Creator and Preserver of the world (Augustine said, incidentally, that preservation is continuous creation) but also causes its destruction. He brings the great rolling life cycles to an end, and is master of death as well as birth, of decay as well as development, of ending as well as beginning. It was the trident of God that the *guru* bore on these occasions; he looked like ascetic followers of Shiva who also customarily carry the trident, either as a staff or symbolically as marks upon their foreheads.

There was some criticism of the *gurupuja* in succeeding years in India. Especially among Western-educated Hindus and among those who had been touched by modernising movements such as the Brahmo Samaj, there was suspicion of the adoration increasingly heaped upon the Acharya. For Christians, Jews and Muslims, for varying reasons, such ceremonial seemed quite inappropriate, many would say blasphemous. But its meaning within the Hindu context needs to be understood.

First, there is not in the Hindu tradition the same sharp divide between God and non-God that we find in the Semitic religious ethos. There is not the same fear of blasphemy.

75

Adoration is given quite frequently to human figures. Thus there is a famous saying:

'Pitṛi devo bhava; mātṛi devo bhava; āchārya devo bhava;' meaning 'Let your father be a god; let your mother be a god; let your teacher be a god'.

No strong distinction was drawn between veneration and worship. In the West, because of doctrinal theory and for various reasons connected with the logic and dynamics of Christian faith, a line is traced, rather heavily and clearly, between the veneration accorded to the saints and the worship accorded to God in Christ. Even the Virgin Mary, so prominent in the Catholic life of devotion, is considered a creature, exalted though she might be, and therefore not an appropriate focus of worship as such. But such lines are not drawn in India. In the Hindu ambience there is a common expression of adoration wherever God is felt to be really present. Thus Westerners often mistake the nature of Hindu ritual in regard to the statues of the God. For the Hindu such a statue is a *locus* of real presence: the God has ritually been, as it were, brought down to reside in the statue. The image is like the host in traditional Catholic Christianity. It has been transubstantiated and empowered by the Divine Being. Often after use it is 'de-powered', unsanctified, and thrown away. But when God is operative in it, then it can be treated as itself divine, as the *locus* of Holy Power.

It is the same with a human being. There are high souls, according to the Hindu mind, who display the working of divine power in them. They are clear manifestations of deity. They are as it were 'taken over' by the Absolute. We have already seen in a previous chapter how Binode achieved a sense of realisation in which he felt the luminous descent of God within him. It was this that gave him the power and confidence to develop his mission. Now he moved to a further stage of self-understanding. He must have reflected upon his own extraordinary career: his many long hours of spiritual struggle and self-mastery as a child and youth; his sacred experiences; his energy in leading others; and now a strange force through which, mysteriously, the God in him impressed visions and extreme devotion upon others. If he was indeed taken over by Divine Power, he was in effect an incarnation of deity and it was therefore important for him to receive adoration from his circle of disciples and then gradually from the wider world. For him it was not a case of vanity or madness. It was obedience to the mighty force which he experienced within himself.

In this he was in line with the Hindu *guru* tradition; similar devotion had been poured upon men of the past such as Shankara, Chaitanya and in more recent years Ramakrishna. He was a focus of some of the intense adoration among the masses which has helped to energise Hindu reform movements. The divine *guru* is like a storehouse of energy which can be transmitted to followers by his touch, his look, his presence. The Acharya Pranavananda was by no means alone in the way he was accorded veneration. He was seen, however, as the Prophet of the Age: the one who was to restore Hinduism in these modern days.

All this gave him a special relationship to the Sangha. As has been said, the Order became an extension of his bodily presence. The adoration by the *sannyasins* and *brahmacharins* who were his followers was a means of distributing his powers through the Order. Towards the end of his life he felt exhausted by this draining of himself. There were, none the less, widespread criticisms of the *gurupuja* ceremonies, which he sought to diminish by the effectiveness of the Sangha's social and political work under his guidance.

The adoration of the *guru* increased rhythmically as the years went by. On the full moon day of February (always an auspicious day in the movement, commemorating the enlightenment experience of Binode), in 1931, the Acharya was venerated with a *lakh* of flowers at Bajitpur, amid the usual devotional chantings and festivities. One follower who had been used to worshipping Krishna asked the Acharya about a severe problem that the new forms of adoration created: he could not reconcile his own impulses with the teaching that the disciples had to worship Shiva and his manifestation, the Acharya. The Acharya replied by pointing to himself.

'Krishna, Shiva and this *murti*,' he said 'are the same.'

The fact that he used the particular term *murti*, usually referring to the statue or image in which God resides, suggested that he was a vehicle of the divine presence. So his acceptance of adoration was not expressed in any arrogant manner: he was as it were the conduit of divine power, and his experience made him think of himself as identical with the Absolute. It is an echo of Hallaj's declaration 'I am the Real' (for which that Muslim mystic was crucified). On the same day the following February the Acharya was processed around eight altars within the precinct of the hermitage at Bajitpur, now growing in splendour, and was ritually venerated by anointing or *abhisheka*, with one hundred and eight jugs of water brought from sacred rivers, pilgrimage places and shrines across India. (One hundred and eight is a significant number in the Hindu tradition.) The monks and other devotees prepared a like number of dishes which were offered to the Acharya and then distributed to the faithful. Such ceremonies often attend Hindu gods and are also applied to the great statue of Gommateshvara, the Jain saint, in Mysore. There were many reverberations of sacred ceremonies from the spiritual traditions of India. The water connected the Acharya to the most potent sacralities of the land of India, and reinforced the message of his movement to reform the Hindu holy places.

During the *Durga-Puja* festival at Banaras the following year, the first of the great celebrations by the Sangha took place. We can imagine the scene – the golden light suffusing the river Ganges and bathing the temples in heat; the *ghats* along the bank crowded with people who had arrived for the festival as well as those specifically there to see the Acharya; the barge anchored in the sacred stream, with a poop and high throne on which the erect, burly figure of the Acharya was seated, glowing in his orange robe, clasping his royal trident.

For the pious Hindus who came to view the event there was not anything absolutely astonishing in the divine claims made on the Acharya's behalf. For them the royal barge floating on the river was part of a sacred, power-laden mosaic. The sun pulsed down its holy power, eye of God, conduit of *Brahman*, beneficent in its scattered rays; the golden haze of the sky and water was the aura of cosmic power and the river itself swept by with its deep, purifying and healing properties, the water of holy life, bearing away in its bosom the little children and holy men and the ashes of ordinary folk; the railway bridge downstream saw the clanking engines of a new power; the barge bearing the *sadhus* and young disciples was one among a thousand craft that floated serenely on the pulsing waters; the orange-clothed *sadhu* with his trident aloft was also, like the sun, a conduit of *Brahman*, an eye of God, a person whose sacred radiations helped to bless the very eye of the beholder. He was a power in the mosaic of powers, a deity in the whole theophany of personal forces with which this cosmos is shot through, a golden sign of grace in the gold glory of a Banaras day. His glorious hair and noble mien had a pride in them, as they were held high, symbols of a new Mother India ready to rescue its ancient past and pour forth its powers in the name of a new freedom and a renewed community. Even the tall minaret of Aurangzeb's mosque seemed to dip a little in the heaving sunlight, ready perhaps to acknowledge a new vitality in Islam's great Indian rival. There would be cries among the crowd of '*Bande Mataram! Guru Maharajki Jai!*' 'Salute to Mother (India), Victory to the *Guru* King!'

Similar displays of veneration of the Acharya were performed at the great pilgrimage fairs; at the great gathering at Prayag (Allahabad), for instance, at the sacred confluence of the Jumna and the Ganges (together with the invisible heavenly river Sarasvati). Also at such fairs and at the headquarters in Calcutta, in Mirjapur Street near to College Square, the Acharya would receive devotees one by one and bless them, sometimes instructing them in the need for self-control and continence. He made use of the piety of his followers and of those who supported the Order as lay people to generate in them a commitment to the ascetic ideals of the Order.

But the essence of the changes which came over the movement as a result of the increased apotheosis of the Acharya was that the Sangha was seen as indissolubly connected with the Divine through the Acharya as the manifestation and channel of the divine Will. It combined the idea, drawn from Buddhism, of the leader as head of the Order and as the source of the spirit pervading the Order, with the Hindu idea of divine power. That power had been revealed to the world both by scriptures and by holy persons: in this case the Vedic ideal was revived in the life of the Acharya. Thus the *dharma* was held by the devotees to flow directly through him into the very marrow and sinew of the Order. So the Sangha was conceived as in communion with the Sangha-Lord, and the monks and other devotees were thought of as drawing sacramental sustenance from the Guru.

In this last respect the concept was different from that of early Buddhism, although the Acharya explicitly compared the new Sangha to the Buddha's: for the latter thought of the essence of the Sangha as a vehicle of teachings and practical rules summed up in the *dharma*. In the case of Swami Pranavananda the Sangha was more oriented to vigorous worldly action stimulated by the power flowing through the figure of the Acharya himself. Nevertheless, there were likenesses between the Buddhist Order and the new one. The Acharya stressed the pious utterance, one of the Three Jewels of Buddhism, *Buddham saranam gacchāmi*. Similarly the members of the Bharat Sevashram Sangha went to the *Guru* for refuge. Moreover, they saw the Buddhist Sangha and their own as somehow organic vibrant entities, implicit with spiritual life, and thereby different from mere organisations of which there had been plenty in Indian history.

Apart from the social-service and educational activities of the Sangha, which were the main focus of early endeavours, were other drives: to reform Hindu holy places, to unite

Hindus politically, to organise religious festivals, to send forth preaching parties devoted to these and other pious aims, and to reconvert Indians to the Hindu way of life. The latter was effected not only by preaching and example, but also by offering a *suddhi*, literally 'purification', or conversion ceremony – as it were a re-baptism. This idea and practice had already been pioneered by the Arya Samaj movement under Dayanand Sarasvati in the previous century, and was now carried forward by the Sangha. Theoretically a Hindu who becomes a Muslim or a Christian loses his or her caste status, and traditional Hinduism had not taken as seriously as the reform movements the question of how a Hindu could rejoin society. All this, for the Sangha, was part of the revival of Hindu national and spiritual consciousness. But care was taken not to press for conversions militantly, and it was usual to invite the local Muslim or Christian leader or priest to witness the *suddhi* ceremonies, which were public and undertaken in the presence of the village elders (predominantly the work of the Sangha in such matters took place in rural settings).

The Sangha, then, was created as an instrument of divine power as it was perceived to flow through Swami Pranavananda. During his lifetime there was no election or ballot, though the Sangha had some kind of printed constitution. It was run on an informal basis as far as possible, and was thus seen as a movement which depended upon an inner spirit of obedience to the Acharya rather than merely as a humane society with charitable aims. This reflected the Acharya's conviction which he expressed as follows:

'For the past twenty five hundred years after the Buddha, India has not known what is a Sangha. Within this period many sects and *maths* (monasteries) and *ashrams* have emerged but none of them is a Sangha. They are all institutions. The Sangha is a living organism like that of a whole man; within it is the living spirit or *atma* that guides the mind and *buddhi* (intellect) and all the limbs, in short the entire body. The Buddha was the spirit or *atma* of his

81

Sangha. By the Buddha's determination and plan, by his inspiration, by his rules and directives, the entire Sangha, fixing its gaze upon the Buddha, was harmoniously marching together at the same pace and of one accord.'

The blend which he effected between Buddhist and Hindu ideals is well brought out in another passage he wrote:

'The children of the Sangha must appear before the country with a new message for the age. It is that undying ideal of the Vedas combined with the missionary and organisational spirit of Buddhism. The ideal of the Sangha must be instilled into the hearts of one and all in the land so that all people are inspired by the mighty message.'

We can perhaps glimpse something of the way the message of the Sangha spread in the first years of its existence through a picture of the period of 1928 to 1929 when the Acharya undertook a massive tour through much of Bengal, Bihar, Orissa and United Provinces (or Uttar Pradesh as the area is now called). A party of preachers would go out in advance to announce his arrival. They would not only make arrangements for his stay in a village or town but would also organise a series of public meetings and ceremonies. The movement had already attracted much attention in the newspapers and his message had particular appeal to students. As his train came steaming into the local station a large crowd would turn out to see him and to escort him to his place of residence. Then would begin a series of rallies. There the Acharya would sit, still for the most part, an object of wonder and curiosity, leaving it to his more eloquent disciples to set forth his plans for the spiritual regeneration of India, through rebuilding life, character and nation. At the house where he stayed in each village or town he would be constantly receiving those who came, one by one, to see and touch him and receive a blessing or a word of advice. The effect on him was exhausting but it impressed those who came to him as expressing individual concern. Consequently stories abounded of his charismatic power. At Hazaribagh in Bihar, for instance, a rather haughty college professor came for audience, somewhat annoyed that he and his intellectual associates could not come in a body to question him – for the unalterable rule was that the Acharya would receive them only one at a time. On entering the room, the professor was thunder-struck by the shining countenance of the Acharya and stood there as if in a trance. The monk who had brought him in roused him and the professor fell down to kiss the feet of the Acharya, with tears in his eyes. The latter blessed him and the professor went out. Without a word to his colleagues he returned home. The following day he and his wife came back for initiation by the Acharya. There had been provision for this through the formation in 1926 of the Sangha Sevak-Sammilani, or association of adherents of the Sangha.

The tour was extensive and everywhere hurried. Its aim was to stimulate the rural masses above all with the urgency of national reconstruction and spiritual awakening. The advance party of preachers, the hurried delivery of pamphlets at colleges, schools and houses, the door-to-door preaching, the organisation of religious rituals and hymn sessions, the public dissemination of the Acharya's desires – such tactics roused great expectations, and yet the Acharya would be soon on his way, leaving a sense of excitement in his wake, and disappointment that the stay could not have been longer. For such an event in the backwoods of these many eastern states was something to cherish in the retrospect of the unhurried, unexciting rhythm of daily life. But it was by such measures that the message of the Sangha could carry across India. The Acharya too was at home in the country. We shall return to this theme later, for it was relevant to his conception of the new nationalism that he was trying to inculcate.

The Sangha then took form and force in the 1920s and early 1930s. Swami Pranavananda was still young but already heavy with his sense of divine destiny. His methods were not without their critics. The worship accorded him by the Sangha attracted hostility from some. The newspapers

83

did not comment altogether favourably on the rising star in Indian religion and politics. Some of his followers were sad and confused in this period, especially in the early 1930s. Could the Acharya resolve their doubts? He is reported on one occasion to have replied with explosive force, as follows:

'I am an instrument in the hand of the Almighty Will! What do I care for the criticisms and scandalisations of the ignorant people! No power can divert me an inch from my path or retard my progress; no, not even if the whole world combines against me. Oceans dry up before me, mountains pulverise at my order, fire becomes as cold as water at my touch; do I do anything myself? no; all that is done, is done by the Almighty Himself through me. I am only to sow the seeds of the Divine Will in the life of the people.'

This ambivalence – the sense of divinity and the sense of being but an instrument of the divine – no doubt accounts, too, for the way that the Acharya spoke of himself both as the Sangha-Lord and as the Sangha-Servant (or *Sangha-Sevak*). At any rate the whole movement stemmed essentially from his own dynamism, from his early days in his parents' house in Bajitpur to the pomp and circumstance of his barge-borne glory in Banaras.

As well as social service and rural improvement, national reconstruction and the reform of holy places were prominent in the agenda of the Sangha. Let us turn first to the latter of these and to the other religious aspects of the Sangha's work.

6
THE HOLY PLACES

One of the main causes championed by Binode was the reform of holy places, for much abuse had developed in the pilgrimage centres of India, especially during the largest of the fairs at such places as Prayag (Allahabad) – fairs known as *kumbh-melas*. The sacred spots of India are innumerable, but the most important are the seven holy cities – Oudh, Mathura, Gaya, Banaras, Ujjain, Hardwar and Dvaraka; the seven holy rivers – the Ganges, Jumna, Sarasvati, Godaveri, Narmada, Indus and Kaveri; and mountains such as Kailasa, Parasnath, Girnar, Abu, Palmi, Chamundi and others. Some sites are sacred to Vishnu, others to Shiva, others to Buddhism and Jainism; some are vital to one sect and some to another. But a place of pilgrimage if important to one group is likely to become venerated by other groups. And so these places become universally significant throughout regions of India or the whole sub-continent. Merit gathers to those who undertake pilgrimage, for it is a sign of devotion to a God and brings one into contact with all kinds of meritorious holy persons. Thus the great fairs – every three years at Prayag with each twelve years having especial importance – are places for the interchange of ideas and spiritual novelties.

But holy places can breed unholy practices. This struck Binode forcibly on his first visit to Gaya, where he was on his way to a cave which had been used by his *guru* for meditation and austerity over a number of years. As he left the railway station (he had travelled from Banaras), he noticed a commotion going on. A pilgrim was being pulled this way and that by a group of touts. These touts had been sent down to the station by some of the professional priests known as *paṇḍas*. The pilgrim's family, standing nearby, told Binode that they had been travelling for three days and were very tired. They needed somewhere to rest. Brahmachari Binode strode over to confront the touts and asked them why they were troubling the pilgrim.

'What has that got to do with you?' one of them retorted. 'He is our *jajman* (client).' They referred to the fact that each pilgrim is supposed to have his rituals during pilgrimage performed by or assisted by a family *paṇḍa*. Records are kept by genealogy, and a worshipper is supposed to employ the same priestly family as his forefathers. But the system often leads to disputed claims between the priests, and through them between their touts.

Binode replied: 'Is this the way you treat your client?'

'It is not your business,' they shouted back. 'We shall do what we like. You shut your mouth.'

The *brahmachari* went on: 'Oh yes, you will do whatever you like? Have you so much courage? Is this an anarchical state?'

By this time they had taken their attention from the pilgrim and were facing Binode in a hostile manner.

'Who are you?' they asked. 'You look like a sadhu: what business have you in our affairs? Clear off: quick. If not . . .'

'If not, what?' retorted the *brahmachari*, and hardened still more. 'Do you want to fight me? I am not afraid.'

Other touts came running, and began rolling up their sleeves, as if for combat. Binode became grim-faced. He looked red and hard but he kept himself calm and under control. He was thinking not of himself but of the unfortunate pilgrim, who was trembling with fear: the intervention of Binode might make things worse for him and they could well turn upon him as the occasion of the confrontation. Fortunately just at that moment there appeared on the scene a good-looking, middle-aged man of rosy complexion, riding in an expensive four-horse carriage. He was luxuriously dressed in the Indian style. He perfumed the whole area around about him; and when he descended elegantly from his vehicle the touts greeted him respectfully and made way for him. He was evidently, thought the *brahmachari*, an aristocratic priest, and he also showed respect for him, greeting him gravely. The newly arrived personage addressed Binode in imperfect Bengali, but proudly:

'What made you come here, *Sadhuji*? We hate to see anyone from outside meddling in our affairs.'

Firm and fearless, Binode replied in broken Hindi, 'How could it be your own affair, *Pandaji*' (it will be noted that he included here the respectful suffix 'ji' to the visitor's priestly office as *panda*) 'when your people are roughly handling pilgrims who are fatigued after a strenuous and long journey? This man and his family are thirsty and hungry. Isn't the treatment they are getting merciless? They need some rest.'

The priest replied: 'The pilgrim will just have to go now to the *panda* of his forefathers. That is what our touts were trying to find out – which *panda* it is that has dealt with his forefathers.' The prince-priest then instructed the man to fetch the genealogical records. As the prince and the touts began to discuss this business among themselves they turned their backs upon Binode and he was left standing there alone. But though he was on his way to perform austerities in the cave in the hills above Gaya that his *guru* had used, he did not want to leave the poor pilgrim and his family to the mercies of these mercenary priests and their agents. It was against his instincts to leave.

As he stood there a man who had been watching the incident from some distance away came up to him. He seemed to be some sort of local politician. He excused himself for not intervening earlier; he had not thought he could really have been of much help. But he had an encouraging message for the young recluse.

'You, *Sadhuji*, ought to take up the matter, as *sadhus* like you have a lot of time. These atrocities ought not to be tolerated: no, never.' The other man was emphatic.

'I understand,' answered Binode. 'I feel distressed. I am wondering what the plight of that poor pilgrim and his family will be. The *pandas'* guest-houses are not very safe. Besides, the whole situation is a mess: that the *pandas* and their touts should be allowed to take advantage of poor pilgrims, and in the name of religion! Surely I will do something about this, but it would be folly to jump into it right away. It needs careful consideration. One must have resources to launch a movement against such atrocities and to meet the aftermath of such intervention.'

The incident was a turning point. Already he was involved with his friends back in Bajitpur in social service: now he determined to add the reformation of the holy places to his programme. It was fairly early in the life of the Bharat Sevashram Sangha, in 1923, that he and his followers responded to what was a truly scandalous event in Gaya.

It was especially sad as Gaya was a most beautiful and meaningful spot for Binode. It combined hallowed association from both the Hindu and Buddhist traditions. A few miles south of that railway station where the confrontation with the touts had occurred stood the shrine of Budh Gaya where the Buddha had attained enlightenment under the sacred *Bodhi* Tree, still an object of deep veneration for countless Buddhist visitors. In legend the city of Gaya was constituted by the body of the Asura Gaya (an *asura* is a kind of anti-god, a god in conflict with the 'good' gods). Gaya was of such marvellously holy power that anyone who even touched him or saw him would be assured of translation to heaven. But Yama, the king of the underworld, in effect the ruler of purgatory, complained that his prison-realm was being emptied through Gaya's magic. The gods agreed to do something about it, and used Gaya's body as an altar to perform a holy sacrifice. For this purpose he lay on the ground, and the gods, including the doughty elephant-headed deity Ganesha so beloved in Hindu legend and ritual, sat on him to keep him there. They pierced his body, Shiva danced on it, other gods held it: but after all that, there was still movement in Gaya's limbs. They realised then what a holy and powerful deity he was and they made a deal whereby he agreed to stay put, at Gaya. The place was named after him and became one of the seven great holy cities of the earth. As for Gaya's power to bring people to heaven, a pilgrim who performs certain ceremonies in Gaya is assured of translation to heaven. In particular he should employ priests to conduct rites for the ultimate welfare of his ancestors. So Gaya is much in demand among Hindus to help their mothers and fathers to share the happiness of heaven. The priests play a crucial role in all this and, as we have seen, have traditional rights to perform ceremonies on behalf of particular families. It is thus in principle a most profitable business. They have to be paid; they run guest-houses for the pilgrims and the latter are dependent on them for protection (and so exploitation) when the holy city is thronged. It is in this context, charming in legend, delightful in sanctity, often sordid and dangerous in earthly reality, that Binode and his associates were called to intervene in the case of the murdered woman devotee.

A certain Jagat Bandhu Paramanik of Kumarkhali village in the Nadia district of Bengal came to Gaya, escorting his widowed sister-in-law Sarojini on her pilgrimage. They found accommodation in one of the Brahmin-run guest houses. One morning she took out her purse to give Jagat Bandhu some cash to go out and buy food for her to cook later in the day. The priest running the guest house saw that she had quite a bit of money and when Jagat Bandhu had left the building he and his people tried to snatch the purse from the widow. She was made of sterner stuff than they had thought and resisted, threatening to report them. So they simply silenced her by killing her in broad daylight. Naturally the police came to take up the matter: but bribes put that right and the murderers were acquitted. The affair became a scandal. Some local citizens, among them two prominent lawyers, took up the cause. But no other group did anything concrete, except the Bharat Sevashram Sangha, which set up a guest house for pilgrims. This sort of work, connected to the reform of the Hindu holy places, became a major item in the Sangha's overall programme.

But the Acharya's methods were cautious. He did not wish to alienate the traditional priestly guardians of the shrines. During this period, in 1924, there was a considerable

89

agitation against the monastic head of a large foundation sixty miles west of Calcutta, at a place called Tarakeshwar. A Banaras Swami, one Vishvananda, led an agitation against the exploitative *brahmin*. Politicians joined in; there was support from Motilal Nehru (Jawaharlal's father) among others. The agitators used Gandhian *satyagraha* or peaceful pressure, and the affair became a *cause célèbre*. The government intervened and hundreds of the non-violent demonstrators joined in. There were rumours that the Acharya might use similar mass demonstrations at Gaya and some local politicians urged such a policy. Swami Purnananda recalls that when he and some other workers went to Budh Gaya to help protect the mass of pilgrims there, the head of the local monastic foundation, a very wealthy man, was unusually courteous. No doubt he felt that the Acharya might use strong tactics against him. But it was not so, for the Acharya was committed to a policy of tact, patience, peace and co-operation so far as possible with the *paṇḍas*. He wished to steer a middle course in all this.

On the other side, a rich priest called Nakphoppa offered to build a rest-house for pilgrims at the cost of 64,000 rupees and give it over to the Acharya. But there was a condition: the pilgrims staying there would have to acknowledge Nak-phoppa as their *paṇḍa*. He would thus get the fees and offerings from them. This would have meant his being enriched at the expense of the other priests. The Acharya turned down what was indeed a tempting offer and tried to subsidise his own work through public subscription. This was not without its problems in years to come. At any rate, he opened up an *ashram* and a rest-house in Gaya and thus offered shelter and protection to pilgrims.

But he was careful to be tactful with the priests, as guardians of the holy places. Two instances indicate this. In September 1928, a top-ranking government official, one B. Dutt, came to Gaya on a pilgrimage from Calcutta. Some differences of opinion arose between him and his priest during the performance of rituals. The final part of these was to take place at the *ashram*. The Acharya happened to be in

Gaya at the time and instructed Swami Purnananda to make ready a room for the purpose. He was also to make sure that the priest was garlanded on arrival and should have a fine, decorated seat to occupy. No-one was to be close by the room, either, lest the priest be embarrassed in case Mr Dutt was loudly critical of his conduct of the earlier rituals. Likewise in 1938 when B. C. Chatterji, a leading barrister of Calcutta, came to Gaya on pilgrimage, he requested the Acharya, not his priest, to give him the traditional blessing after the completion of the rituals. But the Acharya made it clear to him that he was not there to supplant the *paṇḍa* but only to bring about a change in his attitudes towards pilgrims, and so refused. He was optimistic that a change of heart would come over the priests, once they were shown the right way forward, and he was not hostile to the institution of pilgrimage priests as such.

In due course the movement for the reform of the holy places touched other sacred places as well. The Acharya opened up rest-houses in Puri, Banaras and Allahabad. After his death the Sangha also extended this work to Hardwar, Brindaban, Kurukshetra, Navadvip and elsewhere. Thus the Sangha could accommodate thousands of pilgrims who could perform their rituals safely, without risk of exploitation or robbery, and could have orthodox rites carried out economically. They could keep in touch with the holy monks living in such places and perform individual worship, congregational ceremonies, meditation, yoga and other spiritual exercises in peace. They could read and hear the sacred scriptures, and generally feel that they had made peace with the divine Being and brought benefits to themselves, their families and forebears. In short they could achieve what pilgrimage traditionally was meant to achieve without financial or physical harassment. One commentator, a former chief justice of the High Court in Calcutta, remarked that if the Acharya had done nothing else the country would always remain grateful to him for his work in this connection.

Of course the movement attracted opposition. A lot of

money was involved. The opening up of the *ashram* and rest-house in Gaya had the following effect. The Acharya ruled that pilgrims would only pay the brahmins according to their means. One ageing priest, by name Kanhai Lal Dheri, perceived clearly the great influence the Sangha and the rest-house would exercise in due course over the whole financial structure of the holy place and thought it wise to accede to the new system. So he became a popular priest and received more and more income through the *ashram*. Other priests therefore began to follow his example, until virtually the whole of the system was controlled by the Sangha. This state of affairs lasted for over a decade until 1938. The effect on the reputation of Gaya was healthy, and the news that Gaya was now much safer and cheaper to visit attracted even more pilgrims.

During 1938, however, communal antagonism between Biharis and Bengalis played into the hands of the priests. They organised a boycott of the Acharya's system, relying upon anti-Bengali sentiment. They simply refused to perform any rituals for pilgrims recommended by or lodged at the Bharat Sevashram Sangha. When the Acharya heard about this he came at once from Calcutta and invited the priests to come and discuss the affair with him at the *ashram*. Very few came; but he talked to them in conciliatory terms, hoping to persuade them that a boycott of the *ashram* would be against their long-term interests. They made no concessions, however, and the situation became tense. Hundreds of pilgrims were in effect stranded by the boycott. The word was that anyone who co-operated with the Sangha would risk life and limb. Some monks were fearful that fourteen years' good work was about to be wiped out but the Acharya was bold and forthright in declaring that the Sangha was not a widowed institution. Perseverance would win out.

He needed at least one priest who was willing to take a risk. Happily an impoverished *brahmin* called Rathindra Bhattacharya agreed to offer his services to the pilgrims. A dozen pilgrims, escorted by a monk who took an oath not to retaliate if beaten up, were led forth to perform the rituals.

Government police were on hand to safeguard them. The pilgrims, although frightened and the object of abuse and death-threats, performed their rites. This piecemeal defiance of the boycott was repeated and matters continued like this for some time.

The Acharya decided to use public pressure against the priests. He went to Calcutta, gave interviews to the newspapers and described his experiences at Gaya, the terror and exploitation, the anti-Bengali sentiments, the good work of the Sangha, the need for police. The newspapers helped to generate a series of town meetings in which the high-handedness of the pilgrimage priests was denounced. The net result was that Bengali and other pilgrims were fearful of going to Gaya. The boycott in effect produced a counter-boycott. The priests realised that they should effect some compromise. When the Acharya returned they met with him at the *ashram* and the gathering unanimously decided to go back to the terms of the 1924 agreement. The protection of the pilgrims was renewed.

As well as the foundation of rest-houses at various centres, the Sangha organised relief work during the vast festivals which saw millions of pilgrims assembling, above all at the Kumbh-mela held every twelve years at Allahabad. The vast numbers attending such an occasion are an astonishing sight. Ten million human beings converge on the confluence of the sacred rivers, one of which is the fabled underground river Sarasvati which also crosses heaven as the Milky Way. Of all places Prayag is at this season the most sacred. The pious pilgrim should make offerings on the way to Prayag at Gaya, bathe at Prayag, make final offerings at Kurukshetra and if possible die in Banaras. If he or she does all this then rebirth in heaven with the family ancestors is assured. Any offering made to a brahmin in Prayag is multiplied a thousand times because of the sanctity of the place.

The *kumbh-mela* with its vast throngs stuns the imagination. Thousands upon thousands of men and white-clad women stand washing themselves in the healing, purifying waters. Millions camp along the sandy stretches which border the dove-grey waters of the two mighty (earthly) rivers. There are fairgrounds, stalls, sweetmeat sellers, conjurers, entertainers, holy men by the thousand, widows, thieves, brahmins, rich, poor, a whole vast representation of the pullulating life of India: a city temporarily made, a wandering sanctuary of unimaginable proportions. Crime, piety, hope, sickness, devotion, greed, metaphysical argument mingle in the cool February air with the smell of dung burning and the breath of early fog twisting above the waters. It is no wonder that cholera often breaks out among the masses and pneumonia among the old, as well as typhus and other fevers, dysentery, madness – all this woven into the fabric of *bhakti*, chanting, bells, incense, aspiration, heavenly thoughts, and the pleasures of the acquisition of merit. Disorder, stabbings, petty robberies, ethnic quarrels – these and other social ills can disfigure the calm beauty of the setting. There are black patches in the beauty of holiness, and sordid dread amidst the clouds of merit.

The idea of merit is of course central to most Indians' thinking. It expresses the sense of human aspiration to a higher moral and spiritual state, together with closeness to the divine source of power and purity. Pilgrimage is an act that symbolises the transition from ordinary family life to sacred heavenly life. It marks the journey towards the main places where divinity has lit up and empowered the sacred land of India. It is a long journey to gain goodness and strength and family prosperity. But in India the pilgrim cannot gain all this on his own. He relies on priests and his devotion and meditation are helped by the example and advice of the many holy men who throng the sacred sites. Moreover, the pilgrim is not only travelling in space: he or she is controlled by time. There are the sacred times and seasons for gaining substance from the divine shrines and holy spots.

As we have seen, the very popularity of pilgrimage generates its own abuses. The robbery and exploitation associated with the institutions of pilgrimage in the 1920s and 1930s stimulated the Acharya and the Sangha to help in practical ways, by social service and a kind of informal police work, to avert these misfortunes. Thus in successive years they organised relief work not only in Prayag, but in many other centres as well. In 1926 the police superintendent (C. M. Wright Nevile) wrote warmly about the band of helpers under Swami Vijnananda who did social work among the suffering pilgrims at the great Jagannath Car Festival in Puri in Orissa. In 1933 similar sentiments were recorded by a government official at Ujjain, referring to the way that the Sangha had opened a charitable dispensary there and helped pilgrims along the bathing *ghats* and elsewhere. In 1936, the organisation of the congregation of the Kumbh Mela at Allahabad was entrusted to the Sangha and the efficiency of the operation was commended by the officer-in-charge under whom they laboured to control the crowds.

These are a few samples of the good reputation in this sphere that the Sangha gained as it spread its work throughout much of the spiritual life of India. It also helped to stimulate and organise pious observances for the pilgrims. It operated a propaganda campaign through the newspapers and the use of preaching parties to stress the need for reform at the festivals. In all this the Acharya attempted to keep on good terms with the priests even while he was urging them to mend their ways. For he was above all concerned to restore India's former glory and to recall the brahmins as well as others to their ancient ideals. And evidently he considered, being a practical person, that the ordinary Hindu finds the most dramatic expression of his religious life through these pilgrimages. If this institution could be revitalised, so could the whole body of Hinduism, which the Acharya considered to be in a depressed and decayed state. The great glories of the Hindu past needed vigorous revival, and he was to be a chief instrument of this divine work. He also appeared in person at such fairs, and afforded to many pilgrims a *darshan*, or power-laden viewing of holiness. Thus the Sangha was in the forefront of a new kind of Hindu revivalism.

It was in this spirit also that the Acharya decided, in 1928, and in every year thereafter, to celebrate a special *Durga-Puja* at Banaras. The reasons were connected with the various meanings signified by the Goddess. For one thing she is the primal generative energy which lies behind creation. It is an interesting observation that most frequently the female is seen as the source of dynamism in Indian thinking. It is the woman that is the active member of the sexual relationship. These ideas go back to the very earliest symbolisms of human religion, when mother Earth was seen as the matrix out of which growth came and on whose heaving bosom the living vigour of the jungle and the garden spread and multiplied. Secondly, Durga represents a kind of militancy, an awesome strength which crushes opposition and ensures the victory of the Divine. In legend and sculpture she is depicted as riding upon a lion, crushing a demon under her toe, accompanied by a quartet of assistants: Lakshmi, goddess of wealth; the goddess Sarasvati who is Learning; Ganapati the elephant-headed god, favourite of the people and symbol of fortune; and Kartikeya, who is military power. Durga and her attendants sum up the forces which are needed for success, order and happiness in this world – but they are under the command of divine creative Energy. That Energy is Durga. Thirdly, Durga is the consort of Shiva. In her divine relationship she is far away and hard to reach. But like her consort she is also kindly to her devotees. In her form as Parvati she is kindly, auspicious, tender. Through Durga's mercy men and women can draw the powerful substance from her to invigorate their own lives.

Durga on her roaring lion is exuberant, vital, thunderously great: without her energy God himself would be passive, silent, lost in his own ineffable slumber. She is God as Creative Principle. She is rampant through the beauties and terrors of this world; and she is the force that could, for the Acharya, revitalise Hindus in their struggles for reform, freedom and new power. He himself had drawn her power into himself and to her he owed his energy.

Durga can, thus, be thought of as the primeval Energy of

the cosmos in its spiritual, material and social aspects: she helps those who look to her for spiritual blessing to burst through the golden mass of illusion with which this world is flooded, as with sunlight, so that they may reach the light that lies beyond light; she helps those who sincerely call upon her for assistance in material matters to attain prosperity within this world of *maya*; and she serves the powers of this world to keep society together and to seal the solidarity of kingdoms and nations. It was for this last reason that monarchs of old would ceremoniously conduct the *Durga-Puja* to bring cohesion and good fortune to the realm.

There was in such ritual a collective dimension often missing in modern times, or so the Acharya thought. He felt that he could revive Hindu community consciousness by celebrating the festival of the Goddess. It was decided to hold the festival at Banaras. The event was accompanied by seminars of scholars to discuss the ideals of India and the ways towards solidarity in the nation. There were also athletic displays, self-defence exhibitions and contests in the martial arts. An image of the Goddess, gracefully made in clay, was brought out in a great procession, accompanied by the monks of the Sangha and by youths bearing sacred tridents and other warlike symbols, moving to the music of marching bands and sacred groups. It was a display of energy, valour and Indianness and it celebrated a sense of national strength. In the temple of the Goddess her realistic image, illuminated with bright lights, looked down sweetly upon the monks and devotees. In front stood the tall figure of the Acharya, his eyes half closed as he stood ecstatically in front of the Goddess, as if the power emanating from her were throbbing through his very being.

During the ceremonies, which lasted more than three days, there were readings of the seven-hundred verse scripture known as the *Durgā Mahātmyā*, which describes Shakti or Energy and her descent to the earth from time to time to fight against demons and the forces of evil. The Purana or 'Ancient Writing' was no doubt well known to the devotees, since it is used in a number of popular religious functions. It belongs to those writings which are known as *smṛti*, the secondary branch of revelation in the Hindu tradition. They were reputed to have been given in miraculous fashion by gods or revealed to *rishis* or ancient sages. Although technically not as authoritative as the Veda, they inspire merit in those who hear them and are the vehicle of popular religion in the Hindu tradition. It was thus appropriate that in the *Durga-Puja* this especially famous text should have been recited to recall and make present the creative and heroic acts of the Goddess.

According to the myth, the *asuras* or demons once upon a time grew irresistibly powerful. They managed to occupy the kingdom of heaven by driving out the Gods. For more than a hundred years the Gods tried without success to regain their sway over heaven. At long last they went to Brahmā, the great Creator and personification of Brahman, for help. He told them that they could only regain the kingdom by invoking the aid of the Divine Mother. They wanted to know more about her: and Brahmā told them how she was the Cosmic Energy, creating, preserving and destroying the whole cosmos, and how she was within everything including the very hearts of the Gods. He informed them that she would manifest herself in person if only the Gods would unite together in a compact body. They understood the message, and gave up all differences in order to unite in an act of solidarity and warfare against the demonic powers. Strange to say, their determination materialised itself in the form of fire issuing from each God and uniting in a single conflagration which began by degrees to assume the form of the Goddess herself, the Mother of the Cosmos. They venerated her and were blessed by her in return; and so encouraged they were able to take on the demons and to defeat them in a great battle. They were able to reoccupy their kingdom: heaven was theirs once more.

This story was recounted by a sage to King Suratha, who had lost his kingdom and had retreated to a hermitage in the forest in depression. Cheered by the tale, he worshipped Durga and was given strength by her. So he was enabled to regain his empire. The moral was obvious in those days between two World Wars. India was prostrate still, having been conquered in earlier days by Islamic powers and more recently by the British. Only by invoking the Mother could India regain her ancient glory. The Mother stood for all forms of universal energy, including social forces. She was pleased by those who displayed vigour and drive both in individual and social life. She was pleased with the co-ordination of will-power, and this meant co-ordinated work, military strength as a product of a spirit of pride in the past and willingness to sacrifice on behalf of one another among the Hindu people. The message, then, of the *Durga-Puja* was a kind of complement to the work which the Sangha was performing among the holy places and the pilgrims. There the concern was with spiritual needs which must forever be the core of the Hindu faith as of any living religion. The *Durga-Puja* reflected the social and national concerns of the Hindus.

The height of the festival occurred on the fourth day when the Acharya and the image of the Divine Mother were taken in procession down to the holy river. The whole procession was transferred to a line of barges and the ceremony culminated after many hours in the immersion of the image in the water. Thus the presence of the Goddess receded and plunged in the liquid Infinite. But it would remain as an invigorating memory to the masses who could not fail to see the national message contained in this whole demonstration.

Some remarked afterwards how motherly the visage and mien of the Acharya seemed to be throughout the four days, as if indeed he felt the power of the female Energy within him. This was reminiscent of some of the moods of Ramakrishna.

All this was far removed from the spirit of the Acharya's older contemporary, Mahatma Gandhi. Despite the latter's affection for the Gītā he did not have much to do with ritual Hinduism. His mission was mostly ethical, and Truth was a pale thing compared with Durga riding on her lion. His methods were non-violent, and he had no wish to restore

99

some older vision of Hindu monarchy and Hindu society. His pilgrimages were to the sea to make salt, not to Prayag to smear his body with clay. The Acharya by contrast was straight from the throbbing heart of older ritual Hinduism, the Hinduism of power, energy, austerity, yogic achievements, of Durga, Shiva, Vishnu, of the hot Bengal evenings and the sweetmeats of the festivals. The Acharya's Sangha was tough, self-reliant, radiating with ideals for restoring a holy religion as well as binding up the wounds of society through social service.

We cannot fully understand the Durga ceremony nor even the whole conception of restoration of the holy places without seeing that it was part of the Acharya's desire to restore older ideals of Hindu rule and Hindu society. He looked back to Ashoka and other great rulers of the past. It was this vision which led him onwards to an ideology of Hindu unity and self-defence. It led him too to a sense that it was above all in the rural masses that the true heart of the Hindu tradition beat warmly. In a sense he was disillusioned with modernity, for he saw the corrupting effects of foreign education upon some of his contemporaries. Yet in other ways he was fully in the grip of modernity, for despite the distinction he drew between inclusive Hindu nationalism and other forms, he accepted that today social cohesion expresses itself through the national ideal. He saw himself as an incarnation of national energy whose waves the Sangha was to transmit through the body of the Hindu rural masses. The *Durga-Puja* was where a wider pan-Indian audience was available, as in the other major pilgrimage centres where the Sangha did so much good work. So the work itself gave him a national reputation which was beginning to grow, even if so much of his energy was necessarily lavished upon Bengal and its contiguous regions.

7
HINDU UNITY AND THE DHARMA STATE

In the circumstances of India and Bengal in the 1930s, the Acharya's motives and actions took an increasingly political direction. He was still a young man, less than 40, and in his early thirties he had already become widely known through his humanitarian activities. He was popular among young people, especially the student community; pilgrims up and down India had occasion to be grateful to him for his work on their behalf; and his Sangha ran quite a large number of educational establishments where physical and moral nurture were emphasised as well as the spiritual life. But his claim to be a conduit of divinity and the rituals surrounding him, expressing the veneration of his disciples and well-wishers, often stimulated suspicion and hatred. His monks were perturbed by this hostility and urged him to act somehow to re-establish the initiatives he had already undertaken. The result was his deciding to start a new movement for the Readjustment of Hindu Society (Hindu Samaj-Samanwaya Movement). In a reported dialogue from this period, during 1934, the Acharya replied to questions from a monk. Part of this dialogue reveals clearly the scope and meaning of this more political aspect of the Acharya's activities.

Monk: What will be the object of the movement?
Acharya: The object of the movement will be to reorganise, reunite and revitalise the disintegrated and disrupted Hindu masses into a well-knit Hindu society.

Monk: How can this be compatible with the original objects of the Sangha which is non-sectarian in outlook and hence pledged to universal welfare? People will misunderstand the Sangha even more.

Acharya: Why? The Sangha is not going to stop its humanitarian and philanthropic activities to devote all its energy and resources to the service of Hindu society only. We are Hindu monks; propagation of Hinduism and Hindu culture and amelioration of the Hindu society are included in our duties and responsibilities; who dare deny it? Moreover Hinduism is the only religion that does not admit of any stereotyped creed or dogma and the Hindus are the only people that has imbibed and exhibited a spirit of universal toleration and welfare, throughout the history of its national life; and the basic idea of my Hindu Sangathan movement will be to disseminate the ideals and spirit of Hinduism and Hindu culture for promotion of love and fellow-feeling and to create conditions for lasting peace among the warring and worrying peoples of the Earth with the help of the well-organised, well-disciplined and powerful Hindu nation.

Monk: There have been many movements for religious revival and social reform in the Hindu society. Would there be anything original in your movement?

Acharya: Certainly. There have been many religious leaders and social reformers during the last few centuries; but none of them summoned the entire Hindu population under the denomination 'Hindu'. There were leaders to call and organise the followers of Islam as 'Mahomedans' and the followers of Christianity as 'Christians'; but none to call the Hindus as 'Hindu'. Some organised the Brahmo-Samaj, some established Arya-Samaj, while others founded the common political platform of the Indian nation . . .

The Hindus are not so much in need of ideas and ideals as they are in need of strength, unity, organisation, power of self-defence and a will for self-expansion. Ideas and ideals they have enough; they have enough of plans and programmes. But everything has become meaningless for want of strength and energy. The entire Hindu population is to be revitalised by an infusion of tremendous energy.

We can see from this how the Acharya conceived of his own role. As conduit of Divine Energy his sacramental relation to the Sangha had already energised it: beyond the Sangha it would now energise the whole Hindu people. This was putting on a more formal or organisational basis what had already been ritually enacted in the great *Durga-Puja*. But before we describe this new institutional outreach of the Sangha, let us pause to see how the Acharya's sense of national consciousness fitted into the times.

Since the time of the French Revolution the ideal of the nation-State began to spread in ever widening circles. There was first its growth in Western Europe, with the unification of Germany and Italy, then in Eastern Europe with the break-up of the Austro-Hungarian and Ottoman Empires and the restoration of Polish independence. Then came the emergence of nationalism in Asia, Africa, Oceania and elsewhere. The mechanism for the spread of nationalism was empire: it was conquest by alien powers that helped to stimulate, by way of reaction, nationalism in the colonial areas. But both in parts of Europe and in Asia there was something artificial about the nation. It had to be created either through a common language or by a common culture. Often the chief role of intellectuals and artists was to build up a sense of national consciousness. A language, a history, an identity – these had in effect to be created from older materials and traditions.

In India, as the Acharya acknowledged, a crucial role was played by Swami Vivekananda. As the Acharya wrote:

'During the past century, there was none amongst a host of prophets and reformers but Swami Vivekananda who brought before Hindu society a new light of hope and encouragement and a brilliant prospect for the future.'[1]

103

Vivekananda was the most luminous leader in the process of nation-building, helping to formulate and present convincingly the theory that all religions point to the same Truth and that the genius of Hinduism is that it has always known this and it has always managed to put such pluralism into practice and also propagated the ideal. This outlook helped to prepare the way for the ideal of an all-embracing Indian national consciousness in which the Muslims (and of course smaller groups such as Jains, Parsis, Christians and Sikhs) would in effect shelter under the Hindu umbrella. Vivekananda's nationalism could provide both a religious anchorage for Hindu culture, in all its complex multifariousness, and a pluralistic framework for secular Indian nationalism. It was interesting that the Acharya saw Vivekananda's key role. But he himself had a somewhat different view, mainly because as an East Bengali Hindu he was used to being in a minority, and viewed Hindu self-understanding through the lens of the people's fears of Muslim communalism. East Bengal was a part of India where political suspicions were growing as the force of the Indian struggle for independence increased. He therefore tried to combine a certain pluralism with a more specifically Hindu self-consciousness.

In many ways his more militant stance helped to clarify the Hindu position. He recognised that if an Indian nation had to be built up it must be based on a coalition of forces, and primarily with the Muslims. But first Hinduism had to be made self-conscious and given strength and unity. He felt inspired in trying to recreate what he saw as the ideals and glories of ancient Hinduism (in which he included Buddhism, as exhibiting the same cultural heritage). Indianness over the past centuries was primarily represented by the nexus of ideas, rituals and social institutions that came under the loose designation of *Dharma*. This, whether Hindu, Buddhist or Jain, was distinct from the Islamic and Christian values that had come into India more recently. For convenience that *Dharma* could be summed up as Hindu *Dharma*. It was unity based on that ideal which needed, he thought, to be promoted. In a sense his Hindu unity movement was a counterbalance to the Muslim

League of Jinnah which sought a separate, Islamic, Pakistan.

Islam in India dated originally from the series of military expeditions and conquests initiated by Mahmud of Ghazni in the eleventh century. Towards the end of the twelfth century Ikhtiar Khilji had completed the subjugation of Bihar and Bengal, and most of north India was by now under Muslim rule. A century or so later South India too was dominated by Muslim power, and in the fifteenth and sixteenth centuries the power of the great Mughal dynasty was consolidated. The Muslims were often generous patrons of Hindu learning, and made indelible contributions to Indian art, music, architecture, science, gastronomy and piety. Their religious message often fell on eager ears because many of the lower classes and untouchables were alienated from Brahminical teachings and rituals. Also Sufi saints and wandering teachers did much to stir up a warm devotion and a Muslim alternative to the yoga and *bhakti* of the Hindu tradition. Many Hindus therefore turned to embrace Islam. A quarter of the sub-continent became Muslim. And now in more recent times the greatest question was how to combine the faiths in a common Indian nationalism. It was the ideal of Gandhi that these communities, together with the Christians and others, could combine in the pursuit of Truth and of freedom from the British.

Yet in many ways the two religions were antithetical. It was hard to harmonise them except as Kabir and Nanak tried, through a common *bhakti*, a loving adoration and seeking of the One. In other respects there was often deep friction. Hindu processions taking out statues of Vishnu, Durga, or some other representation of the Divine, were offensive to the Muslims who were rigorously aniconic in tradition eschewing all 'idols' and images. Muslims eating beef offended vegetarian Brahmins and cow-venerating peasants alike. Islam attacked caste; many Hindus objected to polygamy. The claims of the Qur'an ran against the thought of the Upanishads, and the divine pretensions of Sanskrit angered the exponents of the Arabic of God's good book. The Prophet was sacrosanct in the eyes of the one faith, and seen as only one religious leader among many in the other. Celebrations of Ramadan disturbed Hindus, and Hindu jollifications at Diwali might disturb some Muslims. The outer forms of the two faiths, then, had much to contest about, and the inner unities that Sufis and Sadhus might discuss in the still of the evening were often invisible in the heat of the processional day. In brief, one religion was unclean and foolish in the eyes of the other and *vice-versa*. So it was not altogether surprising if inter-community riots frequently disfigured the Indian scene. Nor was it surprising if an apprehensive and proud Jinnah should clamour for the pure new land of Pakistan. Naturally, these political claims raised the question of the nature of Hindu unity and Hindu nationality.

There were two main concerns in the Acharya's mind as he sought to create a new organisation to raise Hindu consciousness. One was that the Hindus were divided by caste, regionalism, economic differences and so on. His organisation would strive to overcome such rifts and establish a basis of equality among Hindus. Second, the Hindus were not so much in need of new ideals; of ideas and ideals they had a great richness. Rather, they needed strength and energy. His aim therefore was to infuse vigour into the masses. This was in line with his thinking about the *Durga-Puja*. It was a sacramental means of pouring divine power into the people. His new organisation for Hindu unity likewise was to be a means of energising the rural masses.

The vehicle which he chose was the so-called Hindu-Milan-Mandirs, or Unity Centres for Hindus. He expressed the idea as follows:

'Hindu-Milan-Mandirs . . . are to be set up from village to village and town to town, where the Hindus of all classes and creeds will gather together regularly and occasionally through various religious functions and social welfare activities. This will bring in fellow-feeling, co-operation and cohesion among the Hindu masses . . . The Hindu-Milan-Mandirs will in fact be the centres of religious inspiration, social reform, educational enterprise and cultural propaganda.' (Vedananda, pp. 218–19)

106

We shall see soon what all this meant in practice. Meanwhile the Acharya, who had only just recovered from an illness, set about the details of his new organisation and began an extensive tour to propagate the new ideas through the villages and towns of Bengal, during December and January 1934–5. He included in his trip some of the more impenetrable parts of East Bengal. It is interesting that he preferred the country folk to the townsmen and alluded to the way in which Chaitanya had been accepted by the lower classes, Jesus by fishermen and Krishna by the uncivilised cowherds of Brindaban. The new spirit of Hindu unity that he sought would first find its fervent expression among the village masses: later it could spread to the urban intelligentsia. The progress of his trip, however, was well reported and advertised in the newspapers and was thus brought to the attention of the cities. In February the Acharya returned to Bajitpur and there presided over a mammoth conference, with over 100,000 participants, which passed a number of resolutions about the aims of the movement. Among these were instituting free primary education based on the Unity Centres and bringing the Aboriginals (tribespeople) into the framework of Hindu belief and practice. Emphasis was placed on raising the status of the untouchables.

After this conference, another tour was set in motion, this time rather spectacularly. The Acharya used a large ship, the Kandari, to tour the rivers of Bengal. Hundreds of helpers and monks accompanied him and they would fan out along the banks, with parties of preachers and musicians. The latter would sing songs in the villages glorifying the past, and other workers were detailed to discuss projects of social improvement. Hindu conferences were organised along the route, and Hindu-Milan-Mandirs would be set up in village after village. There were athletic and military displays, as the policy of training members in gymnastics and martial skills was coming to fruition. Vedic sacrifices would be performed, hymns sung and other devotional meetings and exercises promoted. By announcing the schedule of the river-boat in advance and by having the programme printed in the newspapers, the Sangha generated a lot of excitement over the river pilgrimage. It was part of an imaginative series of steps to spread the movement through Bengal, Bihar, Assam, Orissa and the United Provinces. Gradually the movement acquired a pan-Indian outreach.

Although so far the term 'mandir' has been translated 'centre' it more literally means 'temple'. The centres were intended as having a religious function. The idea was that each complex should include a community prayer hall. A Deity would be installed; which one it should be would depend on local decision. The hall would cater for daily rituals, visits to worship the God, communal devotions and readings from the Vedas, Upanishads, Ramayana, Mahabharata and other Hindu scriptures. There would be some kind of meeting hall in which local problems could be discussed at village or town gatherings. There would also be a place for the sacred fire and the performance of havana – this is an invocation of a Deity performed by calling on him by name, placing offerings before the sacred fire and ringing a bell and blowing a conch to summon him (or her). Such a ceremony would be performed on full moon or new moon days and other special, festival occasions. The centre would ideally include a free school for youngsters where, along with the regular curriculum, there would be teaching in the Hindu scriptures, history and ethics. There would be provision for adult classes imparting knowledge of Hinduism and the glorious past and stimulating ideals of social service. There would be a library, a gymnasium, a dispensary and provision for a defence group. The mandirs would thus be centres to unify and consolidate the Hindus of a neighbourhood. It was a modern conception, but it was realised in order to revise a sense of participation in a common and ancient spiritual heritage.

The spreading of the movement in the crucial years from 1934 to 1938 was due to much more than the whirlwind propaganda campaign described above. It was due above all to a systematic way of founding centres in the rural areas. First of all preachers went out in small groups to visit areas

108

where Hindus were in a majority; then having established the organisation they could move on to neighbouring parts where Hindus were in a minority. When a preacher entered a village he first had to approach the leading personalities (perhaps the *panchayat* or local government committee) and explain to them the aims of the movement, emphasizing that the ultimate goal was to uproot communal strife and that no illwill towards Muslims or others was being contemplated – this had to be made as clear as possible to the leaders of these other communities. When the village leaders had agreed that a Hindu-Milan-Mandir could be established and a defence party started, a tentative list of members would be drawn up and a rough census of Hindus and non-Hindus noted down. Then the preacher would take a letter of introduction to the next village and move on, first having got a briefing on the situation there.

In the initial four years about two thousand such village centres were set up in northern and eastern India. They were co-ordinated in sub-divisions, divisions, districts and provinces and linked to the main office of the Sangha in Calcutta. It was an impressive manifestation of a more vigorous and self-conscious Hindu solidarity. But what was the meaning of the defence units which the Acharya had begun to mobilise? Was the movement going to arm the Hindus for communal action against the Muslims? Was the Acharya promoting bitter social divisions? Some of his critics thought so, and necessarily the blending of spiritual practice and athletic militancy attracted suspicion, especially among the Gandhians. To understand the Acharya's position it is helpful to note some of the ideology behind the Mandirs.

Firstly, he considered that it was necessary to restore ancient Hindu conceptions of kingly (but also religious) rule. Naturally the old ideas had to be recast in the modern age. But it was wrong to subordinate the Hindu tradition to the influx of Western values. The Acharya's ideology was traditionalist in spirit, even if his methods of organisation and action were up-to-date. He was concerned with the restoration of Hindu power. Indeed, if there was a conception which was at the heart of his campaigning for Hindu rights it was that of energy: giving back energy to the Hindu people. Secondly, he thought that it was wrong to allow Muslims and Christians to organise and yet fail to generate similar unity among Hindus. Only when the communities recognised each other's strength could they live together in dignity and co-operate in the struggle against the British. We shall later look more fully into his theory of *Dharma Rashtra*, or the Religious State – a different concept, as we shall see, from that of a theocratic state, in which a minority adherent may be deprived of full rights of citizenship. In the meantime, he felt that in Bengal in the late 1930s the Hindus were undergoing oppression largely due to their own divisions, inequalities and social injustices: these were not to be excused but brought to an end through religious, social and ethical teachings as mediated through the network of Hindu Unity Centres.

Although it was often communalism on the part of Muslims that occasioned the setting-up of defence groups in the Hindu villages, the Acharya's preachers were expected to speak against thoughts of revenge. Thus communalism was defined as spreading anger, jealousy or vendettas against other communities and helping one's own community at the expense of others. Hindus were not expected to support this kind of mentality. But conversely an attempt to elevate one's own community, country, race or religion cannot be counted as communalism: it is a right of everyone to promote his pride in his group. Consequently the members of a Unity Centre must forgo any anti-Muslim thoughts: should sectarian feelings, fanaticism or hatred creep into the movement, it would mean the end of Hindu solidarity, for the Hindu spirit is itself one of pluralism and toleration.

Something of the atmosphere of the movement can be gathered from the long oath which members joining the Unity Centres were expected to take. It was as follows:

(1) I shall not indulge in luxury and merriment until I have become fit to protect my religion, my honour and my rights.

(2) I shall not be a party to showy pomp and grandeur until I have become fit to protect the honour of Hindu women and the sanctity of Hindu temples from the clutches of hooligans.

(3) I shall cut down my family expenses to the minimum and contribute more and more to the Milan Mandir fund in both cash and kind.

(4) I shall remain a member of the Milan Mandir and defence party until my last days.

(5) I shall always keep a small *trishul* (trident) with me as a symbol of Hinduism and as a means of self-defence.

(6) I shall protest against, prevent by all means at my disposal, and remedy, any injustice done to any Hindu, even at the cost of my life.

(7) I shall preserve the Hindu way of life, in my food and dress, in my thoughts and expressions.

(8) I shall always maintain the mood of a preacher, so that I can use any opportunity to speak of the glory of Hinduism publicly or privately.

(9) I shall practice my religion in my daily life and will read the scriptures every day.

(10) I shall try to persuade my family members to take the pledge in the same way as I have taken it.

We can see that from 1934 onwards the Hindus, especially in Bengal, would be attracted to the movement for several reasons in what were, for them, uncertain and dangerous days. The advent of a Muslim League ministry in the governance of Bengal and the natural militancy which Jinnah's programme for a separate Muslim state generated aroused a great deal of apprehension where the Hindus found themselves in a minority. There were memories of the controversies over the partition and reunification of Bengal earlier in the century. There were worries in case the tensions would burst out into civil war. There were already bursts of anger over incidents in which it was thought that Muslims were insulting and oppressing Hindus. Especially inflammatory were reports of insults and molestation being inflicted upon Hindu women. Worse than all this was uncertainty over the future. The British were still very much in the mood of ethnic superiority and self-confidence which supported the sinews of the Empire. Yet in Germany and in Japan new, more menacing forces were beginning to draw Britain's attention away from India. Who was to know what the future held in store?

In this atmosphere of change and turbulence, the Acharya stood for a particular kind of Hindu revival. What were the alternatives? On the one hand there were the out-and-out revolutionaries, to whom as we have seen he was in one respect sympathetic, for their courage and vigour impressed him, although in another respect he was not, for he disapproved of their violent methods. On the other hand there was the Congress Party and in particular its espousal, somewhat inconsistent but nevertheless effective, of both the Gandhian programme and the humanist and modernising values of Nehru. For the Acharya there were two defects in the Congress attitude. The non-violent campaign by Gandhi could not really reconstruct Hindu pride after centuries of oppression by foreign religions and cultures. And the methods and spirit of the Congress were, despite all the symbols of Gandhian struggle – the spinning wheel, the white homespun, the Congress cap – essentially Western. The Acharya took a more radically Hindu and traditional course. Thus we see in the seventh element in the oath cited above a hope that his followers would be thoroughly Indian and Hindu in their style of life and in their attitudes. He was fighting on two fronts, both against Islamic submergence of Hindu ideals and against the insidious (as he saw them) effects of Western rule. In fact he was to use quite a number of modern techniques and ideas to organise his movement: although he disliked the flavour of the modern newspaper with its sensationalism and foreign style of political debate, he used it to spread knowledge of his movement. He wished to supplant the dominant influence of the Christian missionaries but his Bharat Sevashram Sangha evolved a modern mode of organisation and propaganda, using

112

English as well as the vernaculars to re-emphasise the glories of the Hindu past. Nevertheless, he saw his mission essentially as restoring older social and political values, and strengthening an ancient order through reforming revival.

To what then did this new Unity movement, which was spreading so effectively through the villages of Bengal and into Bihar and Orissa and Assam, look back? What was the social ideal which was receiving a new injection of energy through the *Durga-Puja* and the defence forces which the Acharya was organising to fend off possible attacks from some of the Muslims? More deeply, what were the religious and political conceptions to which the Acharya turned in his quest for a rebuilt nation of Hindus? The answer can be seen in the following passage from a letter he wrote:

'The children of the Sangha must appear before the country with a new message for the age, comprising the ideal of the Vedic age and the missionary and organisational spirit of Buddhism.'

One of the sources of the Acharya's vision was the figure of Ashoka, India's greatest emperor. During his reign, in the 3rd Century BCE, the Buddhist religion had already spread through his kingdom and his conversion was important to the consolidation of his power. From the edicts which he caused to be engraved on rocks through his kingdom we learn how he regarded all human beings as his children, who looked up to him as father. The virtues to be cultivated were those of self-control, purity of mind, fidelity and gratitude; while the vices to be abstained from were anger, cruelty, pride and jealousy. *Dharma* was to be elevated, and this 'law' or 'truth' was synonymous with discipline, silence, elevation of mind, fearlessness and simplicity. The virtues of Buddhism were thus tapped in the service of political order, which is therefore clearly founded on morality. Although his inspiration was from the Buddha his concern was more ecumenical. Only one of the Rock Edicts is, strictly speaking, Buddhist in content, and he encouraged his subjects to support

113

holy men from different streams of Indian tradition. Looking back from a modern vantage point one might say that he encouraged not only Buddhists but also Jains and those who later were to acquire the name of Hindus. Thus he could write:

> 'Whatsoever meritorious deeds I have done, the people have copied and imitated; whence follows the consequence that growth is now taking place and will further increase, in the virtues of obedience to father and mother, obedience to teachers, reverence to the aged, and kindly treatment of Brahmins and ascetics, of the poor and wretched, yea, even of slaves and servants.' (*Edicts* II, V, VII.)

He began what might be described as the prototype of a welfare State by planting trees, digging wells and providing rest-houses along the highways, and supervised among other things the cultivation of herbs to provide medicines for the sick. He worked at trying to eliminate defects in the judicial system and sent preaching missions abroad, to Sri Lanka and as far as Greece, and to the tribes and border folk as yet not assimilated into Indian society. He was, then, a remarkable example of benevolent and pious rule; and it was to his methods and his incarnation of ethical kingship that the Acharya looked back. Could the ideals and methods of Ashoka be adapted to the emerging future of India?

The Acharya also had in mind the ideals of Hindu kingship based on Vedic texts. Obviously Ashoka drew upon similar inspiration, but the more specifically Vedic tradition had sacramental elements that were also important in the thinking of Swami Pranavananda. In the fourth Veda, the *Atharva*, there is an account of the rites accompanying the installation of a monarch, in which among the invocations is the following, as the king is sprinkled with holy waters:

> 'The heavenly waters, rich in essence, flow joyously and those of the atmosphere and the earth – with the lustre of all these do I sprinkle thee.'

The figures of Indra and Vishnu are called upon, and in response the king takes his oath before the people:

'Between the night I am born and the night I die, whatever good I might have done, my heaven, my life, my progeny, may I be deprived of, if I oppress you.'

As time went on the ceremonial became more complex. It was divided into two parts, one where the different estates of the realm took part in the sprinkling of holy water on the monarch and the other a ritual, priestly anointing immediately before the king took his place on the throne. Thus there was expressed a threefold relationship. The king had a duty to the people and conversely; but the royal duty also included the *Dharma*, which it was his task to uphold. That *Dharma* or divine order was something known to the king and the community because it was based on the authority of the ancient *rishis* or seers through whom the scriptures (originally an oral tradition) were revealed. The king promised not only to treat his nation as a god, but also to mediate and protect the rule of law and ethics. He was thus a *Dharmaraja* and the governance was a *Dharma Rashtra*.

It was this ideal to which Swami Pranavananda looked back. There was a sacramental aspect to it because the *Dharma* was something which had not only an ethical and political meaning but also a ritual significance.

In the Hindu tradition *Dharma* is the cosmic order. It underlies both the material and moral fabric of the universe. As such it is an aspect of divine power, and so is conveyed and expressed not only in moral actions and the performance of mundane duties but also through the religious duties relevant to an individual's class and stage of life. The king himself was an intermediary between the divine and human realms; and although the administration of rites was left to the priestly Brahmins, the king's own life had to form a pattern of symbolic and ritual activity to maintain the virtue and prosperity of the realm. Often kings came to be addressed in religious terms as themselves divine beings.

115

Such sacred kingship formed the central political institution of traditional India both in the subcontinent and in the Hindu-style kingships of South East Asia, where the Indian ideology of kingship took root.

It was to these ideal examples, long vanished, that the Acharya looked. Thus he conceived that a new Indian nation should form such a unified *Dharma Rashtra* embodying similar ideas; a kind of elective monarchy or presidency should be administered in accord with ancient *dharmic* principles and a willingness of the people to achieve unity by overcoming the disfiguring divisions which had so weakened Hindu society. There can be little doubt that his vision was closer to tradition than the syncretic, political ideas which were espoused by the Congress Party and this accounted for the Acharya's ability to recruit loyalty from those who, fearful of the stupefying changes coming over Hindu society, wished to restore national solidarity. It was a natural and important option. We shall later note that by the ironies of history it was more his ideal than Gandhi's which has come to dominate the actual polity of post-independence India, and that it is a blend of Vivekananda's and Pranavananda's ideas that can interpret contemporary India for us, diluted though it is with the Westernism of Nehru.

One of the functions of the Sangha workers in stimulating a new consciousness among the villagers was to hold story-telling sessions in the Unity Centres, in which ancient Hindu glories were celebrated. There was room for talk of Ashoka and the Mauryas, of the Guptas and other great dynasties. There was also room for the telling of more recent tales, notably clustering round the figure of Shivaji, founder of the last of the great Hindu empires, leader of the Marathas in the seventeenth century. He tore away, after many vicissitudes, a great portion of the emperor Aurangzeb's territories in central and western India, and established the Maratha confederacy, which was to remain an important force until British times. Shivaji used guerilla tactics and an army of peasants and fisherfolk to defeat the proud military might of the Mughals. He became a focus of many stories of bravery

116

and chivalry; and he displayed virtues which would naturally commend him to the members of the Hindu Unity movement. He insisted on Spartan discipline, was tolerant, made special provision for the oppressed including the poor and women, generously endowed temples, supported the Vedic tradition and the Brahmanical rules, and defended Hinduism against Islam. Although he was a *shudra* he managed, after some difficulty, to have himself crowned by a *brahmin* willing to bend the rules; and in a glorious and vastly expensive coronation he became the glittering symbol of a renewed Hindu pride. His values indeed matched those of the Acharya, who also stressed physical prowess, austerity, discipline, reverence for the *Dharma*, toleration and social improvement. So the stories of Shivaji, the last, great Hindu warrior king, were a marvellous complement to the evocation of the more ancient glories and ideals of Ashoka and the Vedic monarchical ideology.

The Acharya himself also re-enacted in his own person something of these ancient ideas. From 1932 he took to wearing a kind of royal robe on special occasions. This was modelled on the contents of the visions of Swami Vedananda, to which we already have referred. At his birthday celebrations in 1932 and the following year, his followers garlanded him and fêted him as he displayed himself in his beautiful robe. It was made of homespun Bhagalpur silk, dyed orange. Its neckband and cuffs were bound with lace of gold filigree. When he wore it he sat on a raised throne holding a trident in his right hand while devotees brought offerings of *bel* leaves and flowers and burned incense before him. Of what was he monarch? Did he by wearing this aspire to worldly kingship?

The Buddhist parallel, though transposed here into a Hindu framework, is significant. The Buddha had two courses before him: to become a king, a world-conqueror of a political kind (and that is what his father and family hoped of him) or to become a spiritual world-conqueror. He forsook pomp and glory and became the latter. But this did not prevent him from advising monarchs and rulers, and

117

commenting on the political affairs of his day. Some recent writings, notably Trevor Ling's *The Buddha*, emphasise this socio-political and practical side of the Buddha's teaching. So, although he gave up his own kingly aspirations, he did nevertheless hope that his teaching would help to illuminate and bring order to civil governance. Similarly the Acharya in his own mind seems to have perceived that the old ideal of the *dharmic* ruler needed stressing and reviving, and he himself had a choice either to enter politics directly, like his young nationalist friends, or to keep out, pursuing the spiritual path. He chose the latter but he still wished to influence political thinking from a higher point of view. His donning of the brilliant orange robe signified that the divine communicates to us through monarchs and rulers too. It also signified, of course, that he was himself the monarch of the Sangha (and its servant, for ultimately the king is servant of his people). So the symbolism of the robe was complex, and as we shall see it gave rise to criticisms.

Indeed, it may seem to us still something of a puzzle how a *sannyasi* like Swami Pranavananda, whose food was a few boiled potatoes and rice, whose only drink was water, who slept on a bare wooden cot without a blanket even in the cold nights of winter, who was such a friend of the poor in early days, who himself used to nurse those racked by cholera and other unpleasant diseases, and who stressed social reform and equality, could wear such an expensive and pomp-displaying robe. His usual dress was just two pieces of saffron-coloured cotton material of the cheapest kind. Some of his followers doubted his wisdom in wearing the robe. Newspapers commented on it adversely. Was he beginning to lose his grip? The Acharya hotly refuted the suspicions. He said:

'Who will dare to wear the royal robe, the prerogative of a king? Who does so must be mad or a superman. Am I mad? I declare that whatever has happened in my life occurred at the command of the Supreme Dispenser. If I have done anything by my separate will, it will perish. If on the other hand my wearing of the royal robe has been

118

His Will, then nobody can touch me, even if the whole world opposes my action.' (*Advaitananda*, 1st edn. p. 356).

He felt that his follower's vision, the sense of call, the new phase of what had been a dramatic, spiritual pilgrimage, justified his turning himself into a focus of adoration and political loyalty. There was a strange ambiguity in his sense of glory and his feeling of being merely an instrument of God.

In the 1933 celebrations he was hailed as monarch of the future 'Spiritual Kingdom of Heaven on earth.' For his followers, even after his death, his life was a foretaste of the future coming of royal rule in India, when Hindu glory and the *Dharma* would be restored. The Acharya summed up in his own person these fervent hopes for the future.

The *Dharma Rashtra* ideal went with a more concrete programme. The first step towards achieving a new Hindu rule was the development of *tapasya* and self-training and the manifestation to the world of the patterns of traditional Hindu law and teaching, as a source of inspiration to the whole of humanity. For this purpose it was vital to bring back the Vedas to the forefront of education. Reading them should be made a daily, mandatory practice, as far as possible, and researches into the ancient texts should be made central to intellectual activity. Sanskrit should be promoted as a universal language for India. Its wondrous cadences and majestic rhythms combined precision of terminology with a flexible capacity to form compounds. If its grammar was complex it was no more so than that of other languages which have been and still are being used as vernacular tongues.

Further, in the process of recreating the great Hindu past, people should be taught that politics is not the highest form of life: ministers should be servants, as the name implies, and political policy should be subordinated to the visions and teachings of faith. The ideal would be for a kind of sacred legislature in which seers who have voluntarily embraced poverty and chastity would formulate the laws. It was the vision of an informal theocracy, of an ascetical and spiritual regime. The Acharya also included in his vision the idea of restoring the old *varṇāśrama* scheme of life. This would not only mobilise the youth in self-sacrifice, learning and preparation for family life but also provide older people with ideals of withdrawal and renunciation. Family life would be preserved in its traditional patterns; marriage should be considered a sacred duty. In addition, the holy places of India should be reformed and protected by the State.

This was a vision of ancient Indian ideals projected in a new form into the future. But was it easy to achieve it? The Acharya took a long view. After all, it took more than two hundred years for the Buddha's message to find an Ashoka to put its political ideals into practice. The Acharya thought it might take a hundred or two hundred years from his own lifetime to bring about the ideal Indian political structure. He saw his own work as incarnating the will of Shiva. His wearing of the royal robe was a token that at some time in the future God would wield kingly power: a government system would be formed which would conform to *Dharma* and the will of the Highest. As an avatar of the Supreme Being, the Acharya's task was to make plain the message of the Ultimate: but it was also to set in train a new series of energising events. He would sow the seeds of the *Dharma Rashtra* which was destined to come to India in due course and to set other nations an example of toleration, piety and virtue.

This was in accord with the guiding principle of his thinking, that his own task was to energise Hindu life. His intervention in events would set in train distant and powerful consequences. It was by action that the ideals of the future would be brought into being.

But the Acharya saw, despite this, terrible defects in Hindu society which he thought had grown up since the heroic age of the Epics and the luminous, misty past of the great *rishis*. Chief among these were the canker of untouchability. He therefore instructed the Unity Centres to organise common religious and social functions in the villages in which the untouchables were to be treated equally. He argued that there was a divine element in every person and each individual, therefore, should have reverence from others. He was insistent that nearly all the social injustices in Hindu society were due to the lack of free mixing between people. All castes and classes should mingle together on an equal footing in the Hindu Unity Centres. Egalitarianism and mutual help were preconditions for the resurrection of the true, vibrant, courageous spirit of the Hindus.

To this end he organised defence parties in the villages and towns, especially in East Bengal. There were frightening reports, especially in 1939 and 1940, of cruelty and oppression from the Muslims in parts of Bengal where they held a majority. The Acharya headed an expedition in July and August of 1939 and another in May and June 1940 into East and North Bengal. A village defence army in each area was to be set up, enlisting if possible all able-bodied males from 15 to 60 years of age. He thought that by giving the Hindus the self-confidence and power to stand up to the Muslims, the mobilisation would, despite appearances, bring Hindu-Muslim unity nearer. He said:

'I like to remind the leaders in this connection that even if the much-talked-of Hindu-Muslim unity is established in the political field, still the necessity of reorganising Hindu society will not diminish in the least; the real object of which is to reform and reconstruct the disintegrated Hindu social system and to reorganise and reunite the scattered Hindu masses into a well-compact brotherhood on the basis of Hindu religion and culture. I assure you that in my Hindu organisational work, there is no room for fanaticism or communal hatred. I believe on the contrary that the more the Hindus are organised and united, the more the idea of Hindu-Muslim unity will draw nearer to fulfilment . . .'

In other words, the Acharya was thinking that peace between the two communities was best served by building up a coalition of Hindus and Muslims, and this presupposed that the two communities had their own independence and respective power bases. Friendship, as he put it, could grow between equals but never between a lion and a fox, or a tiger and a lamb.

During the late 1930s the Acharya also developed a series of mammoth conferences on the state of Hinduism. They were designed to clarify the way forward and to energise both intellectuals and the masses in the direction of a restored Hindu body politic. He would preside like a tutelary deity, exalted above the throng, the focus of attention as the channel of power through which God was working out this new quest for liberation. He provided the *darshan*, a substance-giving presence, while his monks preached the virtues of self-reliance, equality, and Hindu revival.

Thus it was that in the late 1930s the Acharya moved his Sangha in a more political direction and tried to set before Bengalis and other Indians the ideal of the *Dharma* State. By mobilising Hindus too literally for self-defence he attracted criticism, but it was all part of the logic of his position, which saw in God the Being who radiates power. He called on Hindus to take this central aspect of their religious heritage seriously. It is put very clearly in a letter reproduced in the little devotional book which the Sangha compiled and published, the *Sangha Geeta*:

'Where there is strength indeed there is salvation. Oh Hindus, have you totally forgotten that you are worshippers and devotees of cosmic power? Behold them, Gods and Goddesses, the Presiding Deities of strength and energy whom you worship and meditate on – how well-equipped with weapons are they! Tell me, does not the fact ever inspire a consciousness of the supreme cosmic strength in you? If not, it follows that all your worship and your devotion have been proceeding on wrong lines. Your gods and goddesses – the presiding divinities of cosmic energy – are not to be propitiated only by offering flowers, fruits, sandal paste and *tulsi* leaves. The weapons with which the deities of your adoration are adorned are

122

the right materials, the proper use of which can win their divine grace . . .' (pp. 186–187).

This was quite a different Hinduism from that of Mahatma Gandhi. But it was consistent with the fusion of political and religious aims implied by the *Dharma* State. There were of course dangers in the message, which is why it is important to note how Ashoka's attitudes figured in the thinking of the Sangha. The Hindu State was to be an open and tolerant one, although built according to the age-old structures of Hindu culture. The Acharya combined militancy with pluralism and so wished to blend toleration with the vigorous self-defence and re-creation of society which he saw as necessary to the advancement of the Hindu cause.

In all this frenzy of activity and organisation, which exhausted the Acharya during these years, the dissemination of Hindu ideas abroad was not forgotten. Missions were established in London and the West Indies. The Sangha was not primarily educational in aim but it undertook extensive schooling projects, especially in rural areas. The Acharya was keen to widen and deepen knowledge, both at home and abroad, of the Hindu heritage. But the Hinduism he and his monks embodied and expressed was not the world-negating variety of Western imagination, nor the individualistic and spiritual quest of many *gurus*. It was a Hinduism demanding social improvement, equality, strength, renewal of a kingly past. It was the golden Hinduism of the great epics; forceful, plural, honourable, aware of *Dharma*, finding power in God, militant, culturally rich. That was the vision. But, as we shall see, he had not that many years to live. Before we move to his final days, let us try to recapture the various dimensions of the faith which he embodied and taught. Let us, in other words, try to get a systematic idea of the differing themes that we find in his life and activities and in the consciousness of his followers.

1 Swami Vedananda, *The Prophet of the Age*, pp. 215–216.

8

THE DIMENSIONS OF THE ACHARYA'S FAITH

It is convenient to depict the pattern and structure of a religious movement by examining its various dimensions – the dimensions of doctrine, myth or sacred narrative, ethics, ritual and practical life, experience and institutional expression. We have noted already how the Acharya was practically oriented and looked to the power of the Divine Being rather than to an elaboration of doctrines about him. Even so, the doctrinal dimension of the movement was not unimportant, although it followed along lines well known to the Hindu tradition. Let us begin, then, with this dimension.

As we have already seen, the young man Binode was impressed by both the formless and the formed aspects of the Divine. But unlike Shankara he did not subordinate the latter to the former. He belongs, therefore, to that stream of Indian philosophical thought known as *Bhedabheda*, which means 'Difference-and-Non-Difference'. There are two sides to the Divine Being; an impersonal, indescribable aspect and a personal dynamic aspect. These are equally real; and the latter is involved in the creative energising of the cosmos. The cosmos is not, as in Shankara, an illusion but rather the sport or play of God. The force whereby God creates is *Shakti* or Energy, conceived, as we have seen, as feminine and personalised as Durga, Shiva's consort.

God is known through the scriptures, which in turn are based on the insights and visions of the *rishis*; and likewise in modern times it is possible for an individual to experience the

Divine Being in his own life. Further, God from time to time restores the understanding of the *Dharma* through descending among human beings. So God can appear in four ways: as ineffable and without form; as personal Creator and Sustainer (and Destroyer); as embodied in the cosmos itself; and as a human being. Although the concept of avatar or 'descent' (roughly meaning incarnation) is primarily found in the Vaishnava tradition, it can also be applied to the Shiva manifestations of the highest here on earth: in this sense the Guru Pranavananda was believed to be an avatar of Shiva. Thus in principle he was omniscient and all-powerful and shared in the attributes of the One God – although in practice God limits himself in descending among us, so that he may instruct and inspire human beings without overwhelming them. There are other ambiguities in the exalted status of the Acharya, as we shall note when we come to delineate the experiential dimension. The cosmos displays the divine energy at work and is, so to speak, God's body, manifesting his (or her) delight in self-expression. The divine penetrates it everywhere but in certain places is more obviously manifest. It also inhabits every soul, who in sharing the indwelling presence of God has a divine dignity.

On matters of rebirth and *karma* the Acharya shared prevailing beliefs, but as many other theistic Hindus he emphasised that life conformed to the dispensation of God's will. He frequently referred to him as the All-Dispenser. This meant in effect that *karma* itself expresses divine providence. Though progress to salvation from the world of *maya*, which can entangle and deceive us, is there as an ideal, there is much stronger emphasis in the Acharya's teachings upon heroic and dispassionate struggle and service in this world. In general, the thrust of his doctrines is towards the practical and as a dynamic pragmatist he is not much worried about setting forth a systematic theology or elaborate Vedanta. If there is one concept in relation to the Transcendent which is dominant it is Energy, *Shakti*. The point of his own incarnation or avatar-hood is that it funnels energy into the Hindu world. This links up with the idea that avatars

125

come to restore the *Dharma*. In his case it was thought of as happening more through energy and the energy-inducing practice of *tapasya* than by teaching: this is a distinction between the style of the Acharya and that of the Buddha, whose ideal he followed in various other respects.

As for the sacred narrative or mythic aspect of the Sangha religion, it is worth pointing first to the symbolic and legendary forms in which God was clothed. The prime emphasis was upon the stories of Shiva and his consort Durga, as we have seen in the ceremonial and outward part of the Acharya's mission. The prominent use of the *Durga Mahatmya* or *Chandi Purana* as a key text for attracting and enlightening the mass of village Hindus is significant, for it links the idea of the descent of God to the descent of the Goddess. In that mythological text the Goddess is seen as descending to earth from time to time to combat demons and evil forces. The whole of the Hindu imagination has been animated by such tales of the way the Divine Being intervenes in earthly affairs in order to restore goodness and the *Dharma*. That is the theory of avatars in the Vaishnava tradition: the Divine Being comes as Rama, Krishna and ten other manifestations. As chaos, disorder, vice and ignorance begin to overwhelm society, the ancient insights and truth are restored. The whole concept of an incarnation of God is more developed in the Vaishnava context, but also occurs, sometimes without using the language of *avatara* or 'descent', in the Shiva tradition. Like many other leaders of modern and classical India, the Acharya wished to synthesise the two streams of myth in an all-embracing appeal to the Hindu imagination.

In myth and story the Sangha monks and their helpers celebrated, for the benefit of their supporters, the glories of the Indian past. They saw the ancient riches of India above all as having their fount and origin in the lives of those mysterious *rishis* of old, who were thought of as having the power of the divine flowing through them, and as the recipients of revelation – the ancient Vedas and other sacred writings being passed on by them after they heard them from a transcendent source. This age of *rishis* and sages gave way

126

to the heroic period depicted by the great epics and the Puranas. This was a noble period of virtue even if evil forces had to be defeated by Krishna, Rama and their divine and human coadjutors. But as we move down through time, passing such noble and towering figures as the Buddha and, much later, Shankara, there is progressive crumbling of the older verities. What is needed is divine revival. The Acharya's followers saw the modern period as showing promises of revival in such figures as Dayananda Sarasvati, the founder of the Arya Samaj, and Swami Vivekananda. What India needed, disintegrated as its culture was through the wounds inflicted by Islam and Britain, was an energiser: such a one appeared as Sangha-Lord, the Jagat-Guru (World-Teacher). As the little book printed by the Sangha to assist its training and devotions says:

'Although he is beyond speech and mind, formless and without attribute, still he incarnates Himself in mortal coil of human body, mind and intellect in this world of us, out of compassion and love for the created beings and for the welfare of the world. This happens not only once or twice, but for immeasurable and unending times.'[1]

So the narrative of India's fortunes, from the *rishis* to these latter days, exhibits hope: Hinduism's energies will be revived. The Acharya has shown the way, so it is believed, and even if the seeds of the *Dharma-Rashtra* which he has sown may take a century or two to burgeon, he has introduced a new energy into the fabric of Hinduism. That, above all, was his mission and function – to act as a kind of sacramental conduit of Divine Energy into the body of Indian life.

This sense of India's history and destiny under the guidance of the Gods tapped the major sacred works and narratives of the tradition. Above all the Vedic hymns were seen as the great repository of truth, although the example of the Buddha and his flair for organisation were also important, as we have seen, to the Acharya. But the real thought-world of the mass of those who followed him, from the villages of Bengal and in the towns and temple precincts of Orissa, Bihar and Uttar Pradesh, was filled with flashing pictures of the exuberant Goddess, of the heroes of the ancient Kuruland, the great light which surrounded Krishna and Vishnu as they appeared to men of old, the serpent-lore and lingam of the mighty ascetic Shiva as he conquered worlds through his crushing austerities, the trident which the God wielded and the tiger upon which the tongue-lashing Goddess rode, the dark mysteries of power-laden Kali, the pilgrimages and monasteries of the magical thinker Shankaracharya, the erotic, divine loves of Chaitanya, and the complex lore of avatars and sacred places, mysterious rivers and distant, holy mountains.

What were the ethical ideals that these doctrines and myths helped to inculcate? Above all the influence of the man himself, Swami Pranavananda, was central. His life was a paradigm of directed energy. There was an inner and an outer aspect to the morality which was to inform the spirit of the Sangha. On the inward side were the virtues of renunciation and spiritual austerity, self-discipline and self-control. On the outward side was the service of humanity, and acting in the capacity not of master but of servant to others. On the former aspect, the Acharya was very insistent upon the astonishing and beneficial properties generated by the power of austerity (*tapasya*). It was repeatedly stressed by his teachings and it is worth dwelling on this side of his life and thinking.

In emphasising the practice of *tapas* he was drawing upon a very ancient and important source in Indian religious thinking. Legend has it that several of the *rishis* practised such effective austerity that they accumulated enough power to threaten the gods, and there are various accounts of how God generates the power to create the universe through *tapas*. Shiva above all was the great ascetic: even so he was once threatened by an ascetic demon who was able by putting his hand on anyone to burn him to ashes. Shiva fled but was saved in this case by Vishnu who tricked the *asura* into putting his hands on his own head. More seri ously, *tapas* was energy-generating and the virtues of austerity were stressed by the Acharya and of course practised in his own life in a remarkable way. So we could regard *tapasya* as the central virtue. It was the way a person could attain a full spirit of renunciation, and thus concentrate in his own person the divine energy.

This energy was to be used on behalf of humanity, and more particularly in raising the life and morale of the Hindu people. The Acharya was especially keen that his monks should provide a fine example not only in inspiring the masses but in arousing many other sadhus and monks, who had too often sunk into a spirit of torpor and corruption. The ideal of the Sangha was selfless service of others in the spirit of the *Gita*: renunciation of the selfish fruits of action. To do this the monk should be strengthened and comforted not just by his own efforts but through calling on the grace of the All-Dispenser and meditating on his earthly manifestation. To give shape to these ethical demands, the Acharya laid down a set of rules for the monks.

First, they should always take 'sattvic' food. This is a reference to the three *guṇas* or attributes of traditional Indian (in particular Sankhya) cosmology. (Sankhya was an account of the evolution of the cosmos according to certain underlying principles and forms one of the six schools of Hindu philosophy, being closely associated with the system known as Yoga.) The three attributes are *sattva* or 'brightness', *rajas* or 'passion' and *tamas* or 'darkness'. They are both material and psychological forces which exist in differing proportions in the whole of the cosmos and in individuals. Out of this theory of three attributes is woven an account of the effect of foods upon our dispositions. Rajasic foods, which are pungent and include flesh, arouse passion; tamasic foods reduce intelligence and pile up weight, and include onions, dark vegetables and mushrooms. Sattvic foods are light and inspire nobility; they include milk, ghee and vegetables. Such a light diet is also simple, and fitted therefore the austere life style of the Sangha.

129

Monks were enjoined, secondly, not to sleep more than four hours. When seated, they had to adopt the lotus posture as far as possible. They had to fight off evil thoughts, especially those leading to sexual fantasies and consequent incontinence. They should practise meditation, repetition of the Lord's name and other spiritual practices; abandon all affections and attachments; and spend three hours a day thinking about the Sangha's ideals and reading the Sangha-Geeta and Hindu scriptures. They should also practise discrimination in bodily matters, particularly reflecting on the nature of death.

These detailed rules helped to shape the ethics of austerity and detachment. It also made the monks follow the example of the Acharya. His long, dark nights in the cemetery, reflecting upon the perishability of all living things, bears fruit in the manner monks are enjoined to gain courage from perpetually thinking vividly about death.

All this self-preparation was to be used on behalf of suffering human beings and for the restoration of India's former glories. In particular service was to be undertaken on behalf of the poorer people and the depressed classes. The Acharya was very keen on inculcating self-respect in people and thought that many criminal and ignorant activities stemmed from its lack. Everyone had a divine heritage, but too many people failed to perceive their own inner dignity and strength. So the task of the Sangha was to build up self-confidence and manliness (a virtue often stressed, by which he meant a kind of inner strength and outer courage).

As far as others were concerned, outside the Sangha, Swami Pranavananda underlined the traditional pattern of the four stages of life, so that a person would pass through the student and householder stages on his way to an old age of detachment and spiritual questing. He upheld older Hindu ideals of marriage, and spoke against the remarriage of widows (then a legislative issue in British India). He stressed chastity among young people. But though a traditionalist in sexual morality, he strongly condemned the inequalities of the caste system and untouchability as practised in modern times.

The ethical attitudes he most admired and commended

were self-control and a tough self-reliance. It was largely because these virtues had been sapped by the imposition of foreign rule, alien education and new luxuries and distractions that he was so committed to a vigorous restoration of an older pattern of Hindu culture. In some respects his teachings in these matters overlapped with those of Gandhi but their mood was very different: his distaste for *satyagraha* arose from his feeling that it perpetuated a passivity in Hindu attitudes which had grown too much under foreign rule.

The ethics of his movement tied in with the narratives of divine power. This concept of power was relevant too to the ritual dimension of his movement. Several strands of worship, ceremonial and individual practice were woven together. One such strand was seen in the great public occasions such as the *Durga-Puja* which we described earlier. This was intended to display symbolically a concept vital to the doctrinal dimension of the movement, the notion of divine power as channelled through the figure of the Acharya for the revitalisation of Hindu India. It also contained in it, through the royal robe and other insignia, a foretaste of kingly restoration of the ancient, Hindu ideal of a political order infused with the spirit of religion and ethics. It signified a kind of Hindu counterpoise to the close intermeshing of mosque and political order implicit in much of Islam.

It exhibited one feature of another strand in the rituals of the Sangha: the public veneration of the *guru*. As we have seen this *gurupuja* attracted criticism from outside the movement but it had its own logic, very characteristic of much in the Hindu mind: if indeed the Acharya had attained enlightenment in which he fully became an instrument of the Divine All-Dispenser, then he was an avatar. Through him his disciples had luminous access to God. That access was furthered and expressed by the cult of the Acharya as more than a leader. Countless figures have attracted such *puja* in the rich and complex history of Indian religion and spirituality. So although not always congenial to Western-

131

educated Indians, it was not all that surprising to the mass of the Acharya's followers.

The main function of ritual in Hinduism in general, and in this instance in particular, is the communication of power. If the *guru* is seen as a storehouse of power – for he has intimate experiential knowledge of the Divine and identification with the Transcendent – and if the primary character of God is his or better *her* manifestation of Energy, then ritual is the means of conveying that power through the *guru* to the faithful.

Individually, therefore, the Sangha monks were urged to meditate on the Acharya and on God as formed (rather than formless), as conveying goodness and ethical energy to themselves: thus they could be helped to combat evil and temptation. Something of the spirit of the Acharya's teachings on these matters of both ethics and meditation can be learned by considering his practical advice as contained in his letters and teachings.

He was demanding in the matter of service. In a letter to Durga Pada on 6th August, 1923, written from Naogaon, East Bengal, he said:

'You must not hesitate to lay down your life (if necessary) to complete the task allotted to you and to fulfil the vow you have taken.'[2]

Similarly, he wrote to Swami Vignananda on 20th February 1925 from Madiripur:

'Unmindful of your rest and comfort, you must be ready to shed your sacred blood drop by drop in the service of your country.'[3]

To Kumud, in October, 1918, he wrote from Bajitpur:

'Where is your self-confidence, that will enable you to reclaim this land? Maybe you will have to pass through many trials but keep your self-respect intact and do not worry. Remember, man is made to face dangers and difficulties. Woes and misfortunes are the usual lot of life and you must never let them overwhelm you. Build your life on the eternal ideals of Hinduism; take the place of the holy Arya *Rishis* and lead this fallen nation on the path of morality and spirituality and proclaim the glory of renunciation, self-discipline, truth and continence.'

He continued to exhort Kumud in another letter:

'Break off your slumber of illusion, be awake to your full consciousness, assume your full stature of strength with the fire of spirituality burning in you and appear thus before the country. You cannot wait any longer. The regeneration of this nation is your great mission. The nation is groaning under the weight of disease, disaster and dismal inertia. You are to come to its rescue with the weapon of discrimination and dispassion in your hand. Stand on your self-consciousness and self-confidence fortified with tremendous energy and enthusiasm.

'Sink all illusions and delusions to the bottom of the ocean of oblivion and be awake with the spirit of self-conscious Self-realisation. So prepared, exhibit your ever-pure spiritual nature and take a firm stand on the most critical front of the battle which is being fought for the regeneration of this devitalised nation.

'Think deeply what tremendous responsibility you have taken upon your shoulders to protect millions and millions of souls. Remember always that your are to soothe the aching hearts of these millions.'[4]

Such an exhortation, such a clarion call to face the battle of life with courage and equanimity, is in direct line with the call of Krishna to Arjuna in the Bhagavad Geeta to stand up and fight, which shows the spirit of Hinduism at its most active and noble. The Acharya hated despondency. Pessimism was not in his character and he wanted his monks to

133

develop a healthy, buoyant approach to life. The theme of his letters is a constant exhortation to heroic action.

'Only once', he wrote in one of his numerous letters, 'does one find himself in a most favourable situation and you must take full advantage of it. Spiritual judgement and an aversion to worldly enjoyment are the mainstays of a man of renunciation. You should be a living embodiment of that spirit.

'To do this prepare yourself first. Acquire the necessary strength and ability. Each of you is a young lion; superhuman strength resides in you. Cultivate a strong conviction that you can do anything. Weakness is the only sin; always be on your guard against it. Very soon you are to take up your stand as ideals for others. Great numbers will build their characters after you. Whatever is possible for man is possible for you. Concentrate on God as much as you can and everything will be clear in course of time. You cannot purify your hearts without concentration on God through *japa* and *dhyana*. And without self-purification spiritual truths are never revealed.

'You have taken upon your shoulders the responsibility of rescuing millions and millions of souls. Their number is a legion whose aching hearts you are to soothe. Prepare your Sangha for that supreme task. Then alone you can give battle to the formidable foe before you. Seize the sharp blade of truth and renunciation: cut asunder the coils of self-delusion and superstition; and thus, as a perfectly free agent, rescue the fallen, succour the distressed, shelter the forlorn, and heal the hearts suffering from spiritual agony. Do your duties heroically and let me pass my days happily watching you working.

'If, as is necessary, a new ideal of *sannyasi* is to be set before the country, then a number of monks like you is to shed every drop of blood to purge away the highly corrupt state prevailing in the country. Forgetting all thoughts of personal ease and comforts, set to work in the supreme cause of the great liberation of the world of men. You are to stimulate activity among the numberless monks of India now lying in stupor, if the stigma that now attaches to their name is to be removed. The more men come in your contact, the more will they be struck and deeply impressed by your wonderful stamina and strength, manliness and mettle, and your tremendous capacity for work. You are heroes on the field of action; you should not waste your time over ordinary matters. A man born has to die and each one shall depart when his term is over.'[5]

'A man displays a good deal of frivolity on many occasions until he is firmly established in wisdom. But those with an unbending resolution prepare to sacrifice their lives for the accomplishment of the tasks they have undertaken and are intent on doing; never part with their patience, endurance and fortitude, nor abandon their self-respect and self-reliance. They never do anything unworthy in a thoughtless manner, out of any casual excitement, or any passing mood or restlessness. Leave aside others' concerns and remember the gravity of your own individual responsibilities and resolve to carry them out in patience, endurance and fortitude.'[6]

On 7th August, 1924, he wrote:

'You are in the midst of a great battle. Fortunately the Supreme Dispenser has granted you the necessary strength and stamina to stand up against blows, miseries, mishaps. Perchance there may be times when, overwhelmed with adverse thoughts, you will feel dejected. Never lose your self-possession at such moments, for it may so happen that many a time you will not be able to measure your own strength, due to ignorance and delusion. Such a state of mind very often visits the lives of all seekers. But you must remain strong in your self-confidence, firm in your self-reliance: and thus strengthened with your sense of self-respect and an inexhaustible store of patience, endurance and fortitude, move on the path of the great Liberation. You must exert such spiritual influence over the whole land that it will create a new awakening on its soil.'[7]

The essence of Karma Yoga lies in total selflessness, as the Acharya instructed Chinta Haran in February, 1927:

'You should deem your labour amply rewarded if, by your untiring exertion, you can bring any pulsation of spiritual life among the neglected and depressed classes of our society. This selfless activity will set free powers latent in you which, in their turn, will be of immense help in the attainment of your personal salvation by stimulating your spirit of renunciation, self-discipline, devotion to truth and divine life in continence. You have devoted your life, under the leadership of the Supreme Dispenser, to a supremely great cause today. Such rare good fortune is only the result of many highly meritorious lives in your previous births. The great and supremely glorious Master of the Universe has allotted to you this task of taking in your lap distressed, downtrodden and miserable people and uplifting them on the path of liberation. Forget all other considerations and devote yourself heart and soul to the discharge of this sacred duty. Banish all weaknesses and fears. Maintain always your own speciality. Intensify your quest for truth and your spirit of renunciation. Preserve your spiritual powers intact by exerting strong disciplinary control over the senses and passions.'[8]

In this extract the Acharya reveals why and how karma yoga can lead to salvation – 'this *selfless activity* will *set free* powers latent in you'. Such powers as these place the disciple on the path of salvation, indeed, on the surest path to it, for self-oblivion in service fosters all spiritual qualities. This is the essence of the Bhagavad Geeta's injunction – work for the sake of the work, not in the hope of reward.'

In a letter dated 26th November, 1925 from Gaya, to Swami Vijnanananda, the Acharya wrote:

'You are (one of the) Hindu *sannyasins* whose intense spiritual energy, born of *tapasya*, was used to invigorate and sustain this holy land and at whose holy touch souls agonising in delusion were cleansed.

'Now has come your opportunity. Very soon through the mercy of the Supreme Dispenser, you shall be able to demolish all ignorance and illusion and self-oblivion. Dash down all tendencies to error and illusion and be wide awake in the consciousness of your true self. Remember the commands and instructions of the great Leader of the Sangha and follow the course laid down by him with unquestioning obedience and a lion's might in your heart. Then shall you see all darkness in you being shattered – the scales falling off your eyes, and your inner soul glowing with self-knowledge under the influence of a keen spiritual judgement and an aversion to all ignorant enjoyments. Then shall you be able to maintain your consciousness and recognise your true self.'[9]

'A Sangha-monk,' he wrote, 'has often to throw himself into the vortex of the struggle of life in the field of action. But the Protector who has given him shelter, guards him always in all circumstances. Sometimes the devoted Sangha-monk forgets his spiritual ideality and then feels utterly helpless. He can get over this if he renews his vow of whole-hearted surrender to his Protector.

'Remember always that you have taken refuge in the grace of the most exalted and powerful divinity personified. Therefore, no weakness or timidity, inertia or cowardice should ever touch you. You need not be worried so much, because you have not committed any serious mistake or offence since you have been entrusted with a grave responsibility. At present you have been engaged in the vast field of action and therefore you should not worry about paltry matters. March on the fixed path with the determination of a hero and the courage of a lion, and victory will be yours.'[10]

Again, writing from B. S. Sangha, Calcutta, he emphasised:

'Many ordeals lie in ambush in the field of action. Without paying heed to those matters, you should go on working with great endeavour and enormous valour. You have been sent there with the whole responsibility of the work. So without any care for honour and dishonour, good or bad treatment, you must work on with unflinching devotion to your responsibility. Sometimes a fellow worker may behave impolitely or rudely without his knowing, but the Sangha-monk should go on discharging his duties unmindful of it.

'Apply yourself heart and soul to perform well the duties and responsibilities which have been entrusted to you. See that the major work is done within the appointed time. Don't pay heed to others' behaviour and treatment.

'To err is human. So it is quite possible for a fellow Sangha-monk to behave improperly through sheer misunderstanding. There are veritable trials for the workers in the field of action. Nothing can be achieved by them if they stoop to think about these small things. The Sangha-monk of your calibre should easily forget all this. The work will suffer if you ponder over these trifling matters.'[11]

From Madhupur he wrote in like manner:

'Sometimes the Sangha-monk may think, "I am living far away from the shelter and blessings of the Sangha-Lord and my distressed and disturbed mind might be calmed if I could reach him, but it is not always possible to go to him". How then will he keep his mind controlled and steady? In that difficult situation he has to think in this way: "There is no such thing as 'near' or 'distant' to Him in whose mercy I have sought refuge. His blessings and mercy are bestowed on the Sangha-monks equally in whatever place, time and condition they live. There must not

138

be any doubt or uncertainty about the blessings and good wishes of the Sangha-Lord which are always conferred equally wherever the Sangha-monks live or move. The Sangha-monk can never be beyond the range of the Sangha-Lord.'"[12]

The life of the Sangha-monk should be one of complete dedication.

'You will soon be going on a preaching mission in various districts of Bengal. Devote eight to ten hours a day to get yourself prepared for the work. You have to present yourself everywhere with such sublime mental attitude and force that people can get inspiration from your company. Recite *Sangha-vani* ten times a day. Every Sangha-monk must commit *Sangha-vani* to memory.'[13]

To one of his despondent monks he wrote:

'Received your letter. No need for you to go through such miserable states of mind. Your fate will surely take a better turn and fortune will smile upon you. Henceforward exert yourself to go on your determined and destined path. Give up all your whims and try to remain unshakable in faith, constant in devotion and with full resignation to your refuge – the Sangha Lord. Then great welfare and contentment of heart will be bestowed on you.'

To another he advised:

'Neutralise the craze for superficial enjoyments by concentrating on the real life through the constant recollection of death. Control the restlessness of the senses and eliminate from your nature all excitement of the passions. A man who can constantly remain alive to the fact that his body may fall at any time, is never subjected to the distracting influence of irrelevant thoughts.

'Weakness, cowardice and unmanliness are the fun-

139

damental sins. Do not fear. March on like a true hero. Do not sleep by day: excessive sleep is bad. One must not shrink from any severity for the accomplishment of a task taken in hand. Any misery and mischance that may come in its wake must be welcomed. It will not do to be perturbed by difficulty. Remain where you are at present and realise that spiritual peace is not always assured in caves and forests. Many a person has been ruined by going there. A strong resolution provides the true seclusion of a mountain cave. Proceed with patience. How many hours are you devoting to work? Is it sufficient to take you to your destination? Think of these as you go on.'[14]

Some of his business letters demonstrate his practical approach and extreme sense of urgency. They reveal the dynamism he brought even to everyday, matter-of-fact problems. Writing from the Eye Department of the Calcutta Medical College, where he went to receive treatment for an inflammation of the eye, he shows his concern for the construction activities launched at his instigation, and his lack of interest in his own condition:

'Of what circumference (with usual depth for that area) can a well be dug with Rs 500/-? And how much would it cost to sink a tube-well? – this I would like to know. It is true that the work or a well or a tube-well can be postponed till the building is completed. But, if a tube-well can be sunk at a nominal cost, say Rs 100/500 and if that tube-well water can be used for building construction, of course, with the approval of the engineer (if the water comes out salty then cement can't be properly mixed), the fetching of water from far can be avoided. Anyway, give me all details. I will be back by Saturday. My eye is all right now.'[15]

From Bajitpur he wrote:

'You informed that the rent of the house opposite to last

140

year's *puja* place is Rs 40. Before we decide for this one we must know: the number of rooms and their size; one storied or two; are there steps to the roof; is the verandah or its side room height enough to hold the Durga image; is there separate water-tap, toilet and kitchen?

'If it does not have enough rooms, can we get the last year house, at least a part? If there is no possibility to celebrate the *puja* in this house, then, look for a proper one and let me know. Write me both places, here as well as at Calcutta.'[16]

From Calcutta:

'The anniversary of Khulna Ashram falls on Tuesday and Wednesday. You and ten other musicians must come to Khulna during that time.

'Travel via Gopal Ganj where you can catch the steam boat. But, if you know a shorter route and more economical too, take that one and reach in time.

'Remember, your group is to maintain the religious atmosphere of the *Asana* by constant singing of God's holy names.

'We need about 500 mds of rice for Bajitpur celebration and Calcutta *ashram*. Is it possible to purchase this amount at Fatepur and Jalilpar, and within 10/12 days? What would be the price? Let me know quickly. After settling up this side I may be at Bajitpur within a week or so.'[17]

The Acharya had a powerful faith in human nature and believed in the 'divine heritage of Man' as propounded in the Upanishads. He refused to subscribe to the common belief that some people can be incorrigible and insisted that every man has some potentialities which he himself may be unaware of; they could be brought out by rousing his subconsciousness through sympathy and understanding. His was the method of persuasion and gentle correction. He used to say:

141

'Do not show a man's faults directly, but put him in such a position that he himself realises them and then begins to mind his ways.'

Once he strongly directed a monk to keep a worker who was a doubtful character in his preaching party and make arrangements so that he would not get a chance to steal anything. He particularly asked the monk not to brand this worker as a thief. His view was that by calling him a thief all chance would be lost of correcting him.

'Treat him like any other person and give him ample opportunity to develop from within his sense of self-respect; his mistake will vanish like a piece of camphor put in the open. Men who fail in life suffer from a lack of self-reliance, self-confidence and self-esteem. It is not a bad thing to feel proud, in a modest way, of one's own capacity. To have self-respect is the first step to manliness and success.'

The Acharya would encourage his workers to develop self-esteem. His vast monastic organisation was sure to have a few workers who would be suffering from feelings of inferiority and lack of self-confidence. But he felt confident these drawbacks would soon be overcome once the worker was treated in the right way and placed in the right atmosphere.

The Acharya saw to it that his disciples went into the world as self-respecting and self-confident workers to preach his message of courage, self-help and self-reliance.

In dealing with people he would impress upon them that they must have a sense of responsibility towards themselves and their country. Before he gave a worker a responsible task, he would call him aside and talk to him.

'I depend upon you for this piece of work. It should not be difficult for you. If the other fellow can do it surely you too can do so. In no respect are you inferior to him, so get on with the job and I am sure you will accomplish it.'

It is interesting to note that many workers with limited calibre have done things with a high degree of success which could not have been expected of them ordinarily. The secret of their success was in the awakened self-consciousness under the Acharya's encouragement and guidance. He placed them automatically on a high standing by the way he spoke to them and the trust he showed them; and they could not help but respond in the best way of which they were capable. Many did suffer from a defeatist mentality and become incapable of doing anything worthwhile. Here is a letter from the Acharya to one of his workers who had become rather pessimistic:

'Due to a lack of self-confidence and self-trust man feels that he is too small and becomes depressed. Get rid of this depression. Always remember that your strength and ability are in no way inferior to anybody.'[18]

Even the most insignificant people can do a great deal if properly treated and encouraged, the Acharya believed. He followed this principle in his dealings with students, monks and the ordinary people. Behind his three main activities, namely, organising the Hindus, reforming pilgrim places and removing untouchability, there stands distinctly the great principle: trust a person and he or she will do wonders.

'As you are a senior worker in the preaching party you should see that disorders do not develop there. You must in all manners assist the Swami who is in charge of the party. If any worker disobeys him, take initiative to make the worker realise his mistake. Do not let any worker criticise another worker . . . a great sin, indeed. Take all precaution not to recur the dissension that once developed between the monks and workers.'[19]

The name of the recipient of this letter has been omitted because he was involved in encouraging disorder in the party. But instead of accusing him directly, Acharya tried to awake his sense of responsibility which might eventually make him wiser.

Another aspect of the practical life of the movement were the devotional hymns sung congregationally in the *ashram* at Bajitpur and elsewhere. The public performance of such acts of worship helped to mobilise the warm piety of the ordinary Hindu as well as members of the Sangha as it developed. Such hymn-singing and scripture-readings formed, as we saw, a regular part of the meetings of the Hindu-Milan-Mandirs in the Bengali countryside and elsewhere.

In addition the Sangha provided ritual and ceremonial opportunities to come into contact with the Acharya, not only at the Hindu conferences held during the latter years of his life but also at the pilgrimage centres such as Allahabad and Gaya and other places where the reform movement for the improvement of the Hindu holy places was most vigorous.

As far as individual practice was concerned the monks were encouraged to repeat the divine name, and to dwell in their minds upon the Acharya. They were also encouraged to see every act of service they performed as part of self-training and worship. Duty is *tapasya*, and *tapasya* is duty: service to humanity is a form of worship, as worship is also a service to humanity. In such ways the ethical side was integrated into the devotional and ritual side. Moreover, worship by definition was contact with the source of Energy, so that the rituals of the faith were a kind of switching-on of the power needed to sustain the ethical and social endeavours of both the individual and the group.

Ritual, of course, ultimately helped to express something of the experiential dimension of the movement and of Binode's own life. As we have already indicated a certain ambiguity, perhaps typical of prophetic spirits, was manifest in his own experience. He had been thunderstruck as a child by the episodes of the *Tulsi* plant and of Durga in the temple. Later, when he experienced the divine descent upon him in his night of enlightenment, he felt both the otherness and the closeness of the Divine Being – otherness because from a human point of view here was the enormous Power behind the whole cosmos pressing upon him. His account of God is replete with the spirit of the numinous – the *mysterium tremendum et fascinans*, the fascinating and awe-inspiring mystery, which also, in a typical Hindu fashion, was experienced as throbbing with supernatural power. On the other hand its Light came to fill him, to pulse within him. He was simultaneously filled and identified with God and an instrument of his All-Dispensing Will. Similarly there was some ambiguity in his teachings about grace and effort: an ambiguity that stemmed from the two-sided character of his experience as a youth. On the one hand, he felt the imprint of grace upon him, as God flooded into his consciousness. On the other hand, his own heroic practice of *tapasya* was single, unaided, unmediated by a *guru*, the expression of his own single-minded efforts. So the enormous energy which he felt arising in him was not due to an external source, but something brought about by him. Thereafter both aspects of experience were to be found in his teachings. The individual was free, never totally corrupted, and could uplift himself through effort. Yet also God in his grace could assist him.

Likewise he urged self-reliance on his monks and more widely on the people of India: but he also showed himself to them as a symbol and concentration of the Divine Power. He was happy to accept the visionary experience of his disciple, which testified to the numinous power of the Acharya himself. The rituals of devotion to him thereafter were a reflection of this testimony to the light and energy that the disciple saw emanating from the figure of the Acharya. But it is unlikely that the latter would have accepted such a witness and such homage if it had not been for his own inner perceptions of the Divine working, as he saw it, in his own soul.

In this connection we also have to recall the *samadhi* experience which he underwent during his stay in Banaras, after his initiation by his *guru*. This non-dual type of consciousness is of course very widely testified to in the Indian tradition. It accounts for the Acharya's conviction that the divine Reality has an ineffable, non-personal side – of which

145

he had intimations already as a child, hence his initial scepticism about the cult of the *Tulsi* plant and the worship of images. The experience of what he took to be the formless Brahman, however, probably convinced him as it has also convinced others of his identity, in some sense, with the Absolute. This is a theme going back to the famous *Tat tvam asi* of the Upanishads: 'That art Thou.' But he set this imageless, pure consciousness of the Absolute alongside the numinous, energy-filled sense of the descent of the Divine, and this accounted for his two-faceted view of the Divine Being, as being both formless and formed, both impersonal and personal. And increasingly it was the latter aspect which came to be important for the Sangha and for the general community of his followers.

By extension the Sangha was his body and the outreach of God in the world, so the monks were encouraged to treat the community itself as a God and rely upon it, merge with it and help it. Thus the differing motifs of ritual, ethics and experience were bound together, it was hoped, in a specially intimate, sacramental whole.

This leads us naturally into a discussion of the institutional or social dimension of the Acharya's faith. A great deal of his energies went into setting up new forms of organisation. As we have noted earlier, he was not keen to create any elaborate bureaucratic machinery or constitutional complexity. He often moved very rapidly indeed from thinking of an idea and putting it into organisational effect. He was attentive to details of finance and administration, though he relied heavily on the vigour and good sense of his followers. The main core of his movement was, of course, the Sangha and in certain ways it was modelled, as the name implies, on the Buddha's Order. But it was regarded as different from other monastic movements and institutions. It was thought of as an energising force, and so it depended upon a sacramental notion, that the power of the *guru*, itself the power of God, would flood through its members and into the wider world. Probably the most interesting of the offshoots of the Acharya's energy was the system of Hindu-Milan-Mandirs, since they were consciously designed to fuse secular and religious activities. One of the problems about Hindu solidarity is that it is not primarily a congregational or tightly-knit religion, and in modern conditions the raising of consciousness towards a kind of national unity requires new institutional arrangements. But the accent remained on a certain informality. There is an interesting passage on this matter in a recorded dialogue from the end of 1934. Swami Pranavananda said, in the course of this:

> 'To take any programme of social reform that would create unmanageable revolutions does not suit the ideals of the Sangha. Hence our work would be to let the life-current flow naturally and uninterruptedly along its traditional channel and to facilitate the same carefully to remove the impediments that have been retarding the progress of the social life in the form of age-long dissipations and superstitions; and in the attempt we should keep our eyes always watchful not to make the society the target of our unsympathetic attacks. Love and service, sympathy and fellow-feeling, friendship and co-operation should be our watchwords in the path . . . Like the body of a man, society is also a living organism and not a machine, lifeless and inert.'[20]

The question could be asked, what society is it that makes a living organism? Here the outreach of the teachings and activities of the Sangha was Indian society as a whole but more particularly the Hindu nation which in a sense the Acharya set out to create. The effect of the words above and the general policy adopted was to raise consciousness through the Mandirs, the conferences, the *Durgapujas* and the village defence armies.

If we are to sum up the dimensions of the Acharya's religion, we can pick out two themes from each of the six. In matters of doctrine, the two major themes are those of Divine Energy and the concept of incarnation. In narrative, there are the stories of Durga and of the Acharya as world-teacher

147

come to restore the *Dharma*. In ethics the emphasis is on austerity and service to humanity. Where ritual is concerned, examples are the *Gurupuja* and the congregational arrangements at the Milan Mandirs. In the dimension of experience two of the most significant are the sense of Descent in the Acharya and the devotional visions of his disciples; while in the matter of institutions, the two major ones are the Sangha and the work towards restoration of Hindu society.

In all this we have an overview of the values of Swami Pranavananda and the Sangha. The shape of the movement was to some degree determined by the historical circumstances of the period. The doctrines and values of the movement were, in part, elements drawn from and developed out of the whole Hindu past and brought to bear upon the threats to the tradition posed on the one hand by a renascent and politically vital Islam – especially in East Bengal from which the Acharya came – and on the other by British rule and its accompanying Western-style education and ideas. Former leaders, such as Ramakrishna, had also reached back into the resources of the tradition but the Acharya uniquely stressed the energising character of austerity and self-control and was alone too in emphasising so strongly the need for re-injecting courage and dignity in the mass of Hindus. We shall later come back to analyse this uniqueness. Meanwhile, we now turn to see the last days of Swami Pranavananda, who was to pass away prematurely in the early part of 1941.

1 *Sangha-Geeta*, pp. 1–2.
2 *Sangha-Geeta*, p. 80.
3 *Sangha-Geeta*, p. 101.
4 *Sangha-Geeta*, letters no. 2, 3, 13 (written to Kumud but re-arranged and edited for the purposes of this book).
5 *Sangha-Geeta*, p. 101. Letter to Swami Vignananda from Madiripur on 20.2.25.
6 *Sangha-Geeta*, p. 59. Letter to Amulya, from Madaripur on 10.7.22.
7 *Sangha-Geeta*, p. 103. Letter to Brahmachari Narayana. From Naogaon, Bajshashi.
8 *Sangha-Geeta*, p. 144. Letter to Chinta Haran, undated.
9 *Sangha-Geeta*, p. 159.
10 *Sangha-Geeta*, p. 78. Letter to Swami Akshayananda from Puri, Orissa, on 1.7.40.

11 *Sangha-Geeta*, Letter no. 14, to Swami Purnananda in Singapur. Written from Calcutta in 1935.
12 *Sangha-Geeta*, p. 91. Letter no. 17, to Swami Sibeshananda from Calcutta on 20.7.38.
13 *Sangha-Geeta*, p. 64. Letter no. 4, to Swami Atmananda from Calcutta on 11.7.27.
14 *Sangha-Geeta*, p. 57. Letter no. 6, to Br. Anukul from Calcutta.
15 *Sangha-Geeta*, p. 39. Letter to Swami Muktananda from Calcutta, 23.6.37.
16 *Sangha-Geeta*, p. 14. Letter to Swami Muktananda from Bajitpur, 8.9.37.
17 *Sangha-Geeta*, p. 9. Letter to Haladhar Sankhari from Calcutta, 12.3.34.
18 *Sangha-Geeta*, p. 140. Letter to Swami Purnananda from Calcutta, 19.7.25.
19 *Sangha-Geeta*, p. 104. Letter no. 49, from Calcutta, 17.11.39.
20 Swami Vedananda, *The Prophet of the Age*, pp. 215–216.

9
LAST DAYS AND RETROSPECT

The years 1938, 1939 and 1940 were very busy indeed. The Hindu Unity Centres were multiplying. There was heavy pressure on the administration of the Sangha, especially because the work of reformation of the pilgrim places was also being vigorously carried out. The Acharya had to pursue his itineraries to ceremonials at the holy cities and in the towns and villages of Bengal. The problem of financing all thse activities became more and more worrying. And like a dark cloud on the horizon, there were the beginnings of real problems about Swami Pranavananda's health.

Part of the difficulty was that he oversaw so much detail himself. For instance, during those last three years four pilgrim houses were under construction, and he sought to supervise the building and the financing of these operations. This was in addition to his duties at the *ashram* in Calcutta and his other money-raising and propaganda activities. He frequently had to be out and about trying to cajole men of influence to help with the financial drive to assist the Hindus in Bengal. Often he would express his worries about the urgency of the situation: 'You all do not realise, but I see clearly that the Hindus in Bengal will die like flies; they will have no place to shelter their heads; they will all be lost. You stand behind me, let me try to help the situation . . .' Then he would be off pressing some business man to donate a room, perhaps, at one of the pilgrim houses. And there was the round of newspaper editors to be made.

Often newspapers were unwilling to print religious news because it does not help to raise money from advertisements.

150

But because of the need to collect contributions, the Acharya was eager to get the activities of the Sangha publicised in the papers. He therefore made it a special point to meet editors and journalists. Just to get one item in a paper might take two or three visits, and with half a dozen dailies in Calcutta this itself was a time-consuming task. Distracting, too, were the daily reports coming into the Sangha headquarters of troubles in the villages of Bengal.

He also spent many hours supervising the work of assistants who went out to various parts of the city to distribute handbills announcing the next big rally and Hindu conference. They would be brought back by him to the *ashram* for their midday meal. Some asked whether he was not wasting time seeing to such relatively minor matters, but his motto was that no work is small, and his leadership and enthusiasm improved the effectiveness of these task-forces. But it was wearing; and he ate little – a handful of rice or parched *gram* and half an orange. If a senior monk offered to cook for him he would send him off to do something more vital. If it were a younger monk he would upbraid him. Work was what was important, not trying to please the Acharya. He would often be impatient about personal problems put to him, as if all that mattered was getting on speedily with the work of the cause, and as if he really had little time left to complete his mission. These were fraught and anxious days. Members of his entourage, frightened a little by his manner – for he occasionally had an outburst of anger at being interrupted in his labours – were reluctant to trouble him with their own worries and concerns.

Despite signs of trouble with his health, he was amazingly active. He would be on the go from 3 o'clock in the morning until after midnight. He might not close the door to his room until 1 or 2 a.m. but at 3 a.m. he would be up again with the words: 'I do not take rest; how can you stay in bed? Get up, we are like soldiers on the battlefield. We just can't afford any rest.' His eagerness for work was partly due to the hope of overcoming disappointment at the rather apathetic attitude of rich people towards the Hindu unity movement.

He felt keenly the financial stringency hobbling his organisation.

Once it happened that one of the monks was rebuffed by a rich man when he went to him for money. Hearing about it, and in the light of other somewhat disheartening news of the same kind, the Acharya gave way to some strong feelings:

'Now I see why some political workers have left the field-work for want of money. Nobody wants to dip his hand into his pocket to encourage those who shed their blood for their country and community, though numberless people roll in luxury and plenty. I need thousands of workers to organise the Hindus, but where is the finance for them? I have tried my best with rich people but they just do not listen. Numberless religious estates own heaps of money, but not a penny for preaching and propagating the Hindu religion. Sometimes I feel like selling the Calcutta *ashram* building and spending away the proceeds in Hindu organisational works . . .'

Some monks about this time made a revolutionary suggestion which attracted the Acharya's wrath. They suggested that the financial crisis could be overcome by working miracles. He retorted:

'Solving money problems by miracles is no less than earning money by prostitution. Should yogic achievements that are meant to spread spiritual ideals in the country be spent for such common things as raising funds? Shame. No Acharya has ever done this nor will it ever be done.'[1]

His health was deteriorating. He had contracted diabetes, and although part of the treatment was the reduction of food – and fasting of course suited his temperament – he took food only irregularly and on occasions would go for a whole day without eating. This did not improve his condition. He eventually came down with beriberi, accompanied by a continuing high fever. His feet became swollen. A physician who examined him was thoroughly alarmed and urged him to stay in Calcutta to rest. He asked the Acharya whether he was trying to kill himself with this perpetual activity when he was a seriously sick man. Better to stay put in Calcutta and undergo systematic treatment. After a long time the beriberi wore off. In the meantime, however, he contracted glaucoma, and his eyesight worsened. He also began to lose sensation in his feet, possibly due to some dietary deficiency, and blisters developed on the soles of his feet which turned into sores, since he would not give up walking. He sensed a coming crisis, but rejected suggestions for prolonged treatment and going to a health resort with the words:

'Whether my legs and eyes survive or not, I do not care. I have no time for all this now. When I am totally confined, then I shall see . . .'[2]

In view of his sickness, his activity was phenomenal and the seriousness of his condition was only apparent to those closest to him. After all, he was on the move from one state to another, sometimes in connection with the building of the pilgrim guest houses, sometimes in connection with Hindu conferences and for ceremonies commemorating the foundation of the various *ashrams*, accompanied always by a small army of monks and workers laden like an army with all sorts of impedimenta and going off into the villages to provide protection for the oppressed and hope for the future. He may have been sick and occasionally downcast at the lack of response among the middle classes and opposition from some Congress politicians. But he must have felt satisfaction at the degree to which his movement had spread, and at the evident welcome of the crowds that came to see him. He still looked burly, his face still had that calm mien which spoke volumes for his ideals of mediating between heaven and earth; and his garb and escort made him majestic. Who was to know that he was getting worn down by detail, by the immense burden of simultaneously being administrator of so

153

much and pastor of so many? From a worldly, rational perspective no doubt he should not have dealt with the smaller matters that filled so much of his days; but he had an organic relationship to the Sangha which sucked him into the whirlpool of hectic endeavours and complex demands. On looking at him from afar, people could not see that he was ailing. Even those close to him could not fail to be overawed by his continuing energy, even as his body, so magnificent once, began to suffer from severe troubles.

In late October 1940 he decided to go to Banaras. These were dramatic times. In far-off Europe the war had exploded in earnest that spring and summer. The Germans had been fought off over the Channel, but England was in deep trouble in the Middle East. She was half-isolated from her Indian Empire. Surely these events portended changes in India. Patriots could not fail to hope for a fresh impetus to the independence struggle; and yet this also brought tremors to the surface of Hindu-Muslim relations. The Acharya, however, was perhaps beginning to see that his own mission was closing and that it would have to be the Sangha that projected forwards the energies which he had released. His desire to go to Banaras had a special meaning for him, at any rate, as events were to show. From the *ashram* he went in some pomp to the Temple of Vishvanath.

This temple, close by the Dasasvamedha Ghat or the Steps of the Ten Horse Sacrifice, was one of the most holy buildings of Banaras, dedicated to Shiva as Lord of All. It was hereabouts that, according to legend, Brahmā had performed the sacrifice of ten horses in order to sanctify the city even more than its sister city of Prayag, where he had performed a sacrifice to celebrate the return of the lost Vedas. For pious Hindus the Vishvanath Temple was a reminder of the vicissitudes of conquest – it had been destroyed a number of times by the Muslims and rebuilt. It was here that the Acharya wished to go, in ceremonious fashion, to call upon the great Lord of the Universe. No doubt there ran through his mind scenes from his young manhood when he had frequented the *ghats* in meditation on

154

death and on the eternal, gazed with wonder at the golden roof of the temple and the rose-blue sky of evening and drunk in the smells of the city and the distant sounds of hymn-singing. Now he was coming here as a famous man, and in a car, which he took as far as the end of the lane that led down to the Temple. He was escorted like royalty. On either side of him were the robust young men of the Hindu defence corps. Beneath his feet was spread a beautiful, saffron cloth embroidered with lotuses. When he had paced one length of cloth another would be brought for the next stretch. A velvet umbrella with silver tassels and needlework was held over his head. Ornamental velvet fans were waved about him, and sacred yak tails. He paced slowly onwards, thus marked with the accoutrements of divinity, for all the world like one God going to call ceremoniously upon another. In these last years he had rarely entered a regular temple but had frequented rather the altars and prayer halls of the movement's *ashrams*. He entered the temple by one door, and stood there with half-closed eyes, while the chief temple priest hung a garland about his neck. He seemed to be present in the temple and yet at the same time inwardly withdrawn. Without a word and just as slowly and quietly as he had come he left by another door and paced back to his car, again attended with pomp. He did not explain this mysterious visit, so heavy with atmosphere and so brief. What was the meaning of the cloth strewed thus on the ground? He used to have this set out when he went to sit on his altars in the *ashrams*, to receive the adoration of his followers. It was as if he went into a Temple that he regarded somehow as his own.

After this event there was a clear change in his behaviour. Hence it was thought by his followers that the visit to the Vishvanath Temple marked a decision or recognition by him of the impending end, as he conceived it, of his earthly mission. He began to be more detached. As we have seen, if he had a fault it was in overseeing in too close detail the work of his monks. He had a clear and inquisitive eye for all manner of detail. Now he would often say: 'Do as you think best,' or 'Do it if you think it is proper'. He even remarked:

155

'Have I left anything undone? Bit by bit I have given myself away freely in the Sangha'. He had always been so keen on supervising everything, even on big occasions. Now he was giving the members of the Sangha their head. It could be that he needed to give them greater freedom if they were to carry on his work after he was gone. At any rate he was now cool in many matters about which he would previously have been ardently concerned. It was a shock to some of his closest and most devoted disciples. They had for so long lived with him as their leader, friend, god. They had treated him with affection and reverence and he had responded with vigour and tenderness. One of the monks, Swami Vedananda expressed his feelings like this:[3]

'At last the time of great transformation was approaching. I began to feel at heart that Acharya's physique was no longer able to hold him in its frame. But that the divine vessel whose soothing nectar of unending love, care, mercy and forgiveness had brought me up for the last twenty-two years, had protected me from the fire and fever of *samsara* and made me free from the poison of worldliness accumulated from many incarnations, might be out of our sight – such thoughts of such a tragedy began to pain, to agonise me and make me most fearful. Like children we unhesitatingly sat on his lap, rested on his breast, took food from his hand, sang before him with sentiment and gratitude, fanned him, cooked his food, served him, opened our hearts to him, took his teachings in, worshipped him, received directives at every step – in so many ways are we indebted to him through his physical existence. Now in the absence of that physical personality, how could we survive? How could we carry on?

'But the inevitable is unavoidable. The consolation was found too. The Acharya himself announced, the Sangha and Sangha-Lord are inseparable. The Sangha is the vaster body of the Sangha-Lord. Why disappointment then? Melancholy? But this solace in some of us took a slightly ugly turn. It was unbecoming of us sometimes to think that we could now well manage the affairs of the Sangha without receiving directions from Acharya.'[4]

The outpouring of sentiment in this passage is quite remarkable. We may note that the whole procedure of feeding the Acharya, of dressing him, and so forth followed the pattern typical in temple worship in India where the image of the God or Goddess is treated as if it were a human, being, woken up in the morning, bathed, fed and taken through the rhythms of the day. It is a testimony to the disciples' sense of the numinous graciousness of the Acharya's personality that they could thus with reverence and affection treat him as their adopted God. They saw in this big, tender, majestic, decisive human being – even in his last days when his body was beginning to disintegrate – the real presence of the Divine Power sustaining the cosmos. It is not an attitude that comes naturally to those brought up in the Western tradition or in the Jewish, Christian or Islamic faiths. But it reflects a Hindu capacity to visualise deity in many forms and here in the form of an avatar of Shiva. Because it was through such rituals that the *guru* was bound to his Sangha, the actual, impending disappearance of the teacher and divine friend was felt as hard to conceive of and hard to bear.

In December he decided to set off from Calcutta on another of his great journeys into the hinterland of Bengal. At his first stop, which was at Jalpaiguri, he had a typically strenuous day. From 7.30 until 10 o'clock in the morning he was sitting in an open car being taken in procession round the town. In the afternoon he attended an open air public meeting which was held in the courtyard of the Arya-Natya-Samaj (Aryan Dance Society) from 5 in the evening until 9 o'clock at night. He again attended public functions, lectures and a sacrificial ritual lasting about four hours. He did not miss the smaller meetings either. The next halt was at Dinajpur, which the train reached at 3 o'clock in the morning of the 18th of December. He decided to stay for the rest of the night at the station, since in the early morning a great proces-

157

sion was to start from there: it would have been too hasty and disturbing to rush into town for a rest. The parade turned out to be of great length and lasted two hours. He was also at the public meeting scheduled for that afternoon and lasting until about 8.30 p.m. Every hour his physical condition became alarmingly worse. He found it hard to drag his body along and only sustained these public events by merciless application of his will. He was due next at Rangpur, although it was becoming more and more obvious that he could tolerate no more travel or public functions. But he made it to Rangpur, where an unexpectedly huge reception was awaiting him at the station. Thousands of people accompanied his car in a slow procession into the town, a distance of about three miles. He was propped up in a sitting position in the car, his head resting on a pillow, holding his *sannyasin*'s staff in his right hand. On arriving at the residence where he was to stay he took to bed and could not attend anything else at Rangpur. At last he gave permission to turn back, and with his agreement the rest of the tour (to Rajshahi, Pabna and Bogura) was cancelled. He had asked his doctor for medicine to stimulate his heart so that he could in fact carry on, but the physician's refusal put an end to any further thought of going on with the journey.

On December 23rd he got back to Calcutta. He was carried into the *ashram* and lay on his bed. He remained quiet for a while, then clenched and unclenched his hand repeatedly. This was a habit that he sometimes displayed when he was satisfied with himself.

He breathed a deep sigh of relief and then said to no-one in particular: 'Enough! I could not possibly have done more. Building up such a big organisation is easy? These days? Oh, very hard indeed!' Then, turning to the monks who were there, he said: 'All of you are quite fit now, are you not?' A mark of contentment was very obvious on his countenance.[5]

He was asked whether the monks who had nursed him earlier should be sent for (they were out of Calcutta), but he answered in the negative. He did not want any monk who might be on some duty out of Calcutta, not even Swami

Satchidananda, who was to succeed him as President of the Sangha, to leave the task entrusted to him in order to stay by his bedside just because he, their *guru*, was sick. He did not, even in this hour of crisis, make allowance for sentiment. He must carry on; and they too, however strong their bond of affection to him, should carry on.

The monks there at the *ashram* looked after him in these last days. One recorded in his diary how he was afraid he might by any chance be away at the time of the Acharya's death and only read about it in the newspapers from afar: but the Acharya kept him with him throughout. Hundreds of followers came to the *ashram* in Ballyganj to keep vigil and to pray for his recovery. But he contracted pneumonia as well as his other ailments. On 8 January 1941, at 12.45 a.m. he expired. He passed away with a smile of peace on his lips. He was less than 45 years old. Considering his earlier physique, it was a surprisingly early end. But he had crowded a lot into the years he had at his disposal.

He had had a vault for the reception of his body built at Bajitpur. His body was carried back there, to the altar where he had first felt the descent of the Divine Being into his own person, now the centre of the whole cult and of the spiritual movement he had directed. Thousands came for a final *darshan*, drawing substance even in death from the holy leader. His body was bathed in the holy water close by the Siddha Peetha, as the altar was called, and in due course with proper ritual his body was lowered into the prepared vault.

Hindus usually burn the dead but *sannyasins* and other holy persons (and little babies) are not cremated. This symbolises that they are beyond society and exist on a higher social and spiritual plane. It may also reflect customs going back to the primeval past before the Aryans even came to India. The monks of the Sangha solemnly consigned his body to the earth, while crowds chanted the sacred formula *'Hare Ram Hare Ram, Ram, Ram, Hare, Hare'*. Thus the person who, they believed, incarnated Shiva's Energy was sent on his way to nirvana with the chants of Vishnu and his avatars.

The monks, so dependent on him, were devastated at first by having the central person of the Sangha taken away. But there still remained the Order as the visible manifestation of the Acharya and they turned their efforts to maintaining and extending its work. Meanwhile mysterious visionary events occurred which it is well to record here as testimony which helped to infuse life into the followers. Whatever we make of these stories, they express something important about the kind of devotion which Swami Pranavananda attracted. They are stories which fed the ongoing devotion which the Sangha and other disciples focused on the Acharya.

An old woman devotee who lived in the village of Antpur in the Hooghly district, about thirty miles away from Calcutta, had heard the news of the Acharya's death and hurried to pay her respects to the body. But by the time she had reached Calcutta the corpse had already been taken to Bajitpur. Crazed with grief and by her failure to reach him in time, she rushed to the river Ganges in order to throw herself in.

At that point the Acharya appeared in front of her and, taking her by the hand, said to her, 'Dear child, how is it that you are going to kill yourself? Did I not tell you time and again that I am always with you? Don't you see me as before?' He led her up to the tram route, seated her in a tram car and vanished.

She came back to the *ashram* weeping, saying: 'Ah, misfortune! The Acharya gave me *darshan* but sinner as I am I have lost sight of him again.'[6]

Another piece of testimony was this. A disciple of the Acharya, Swami Sureswarananda, who now and then had cooked for him during the great Jagannath festival at Puri in Orissa, while he was staying at the Puri Ashram, went to market one day in July with Swami Advaitananda, to buy some fruits to offer at the altar of the Acharya. He admitted to scepticism to his brother monk.

'What value is there in *puja* or in offering food to the Deity?'

Swami Advaitananda rebuked him for such disbelief in the

160

omnipresence of the great *guru*. But Sureswarananda repeated his disbelief. He complained that he got no response to his prayers and veneration. He was lax in making his offerings before the portrait of the Acharya which was on the altar. It is a common feature of the Hindu tradition to use such portraits as immediate objects of reverence and to treat them as one would the actual deities and *gurus* whom they venerate. One night the Acharya appeared to the doubtful Swami in a dream, saying that the Swami had been quite keen on arranging for his own food and bed, but nothing had been done for him, the Acharya. The Swami dismissed it as a mere dream, but had the same vision twice more that night, and after that became attentive to the duty of making offerings.

Swami Vedananda, who wrote a sketch of the life of the Acharya, had completed the edition of the book in Bengali and one night dreamed that the Acharya came to him in any angry mood, bearing a trident in his hand. He berated the Swami for writing about his passing away. How could he die? Swami Vedananda woke up and fell down begging the Acharya's forgiveness. He spent the rest of the night in meditation and in the morning he went to the press and had the last chapter destroyed. He added a page of prayer for mercy at the end of the edition. (However, the English edition includes an account of the Acharya's death but adds accounts of these 'resurrection' narratives.)

Another incident recorded during that period was about the son of a certain Rabindra Hore, a Kayastha landlord of the district of Pabna in Bengal. His wife was a loyal devotee of the Acharya and regularly made food offerings before the picture of Swami Pranavananda. While she performed the rites, her nephew, a little boy of five, would sit by her side, his eyes closed. One day not long after the death of the *guru*, she had finished the rituals and had gone out to fetch something else, when she heard a cry from the room: 'Quick, quick, aunt, quick!' When she had hurried back into the little prayer room, the boy told her in a trembling voice that he had seen the Deity come down out of the picture and start to partake of the food, and he had been frightened.

161

One or two other dramatic incidents are recounted of miraculous help received from the Acharya after his death. What do these testimonies signify? The important point to recognise from the perspective of the history and scientific study of religion is that these visionary experiences are part of a larger pattern of devotional faith which, from the standpoint of the faithful, undoubtedly brought life-giving power into their lives. The faithful follower of the Acharya would feel that somehow behind and through all the happenings of his daily life he and other devotees could see the unseen hand of the *guru*. They could sense his force behind their own experience of conversion and illumination; they could feel it too in their ever-increasing sense of dedication, in the turn of events to protect them from spiritual adversity and in the sense of support received even in distant parts of the globe in times of trial and distress; and they could note how even unsuccessful followers received guidance and help. Such feelings animate the faithful, and it is from them that the movement set in train by the Acharya draws its sustenance.

In trying to bring out the meaning of events from within, we need to put on one side for the moment the rationalistic scepticism which the modern observer might feel. Can we not explain all the events described above as consequences of natural forces – the projective spirit of human imagination or the arm of coincidence? But it is typical of religion everywhere to treat natural events from what the faithful regard as a deeper perspective, in which the guiding power of the Divine is evident. The same event can be merely coincidental to one person, highly meaningful to another. Our task here has been to set forth the Acharya's career in part at least from the perspective of those whose lives he energised. And the *post mortem* appearances are important to record, as they provide both an insight into the way his power continued after death and part of the testimony upon which the movement continues to call in pointing to the luminous character of the leader's life.

Finally, it is important for us to look back in retrospect

162

upon the career of this remarkable man and put it into a wider perspective. It is convenient first of all to comment on his place in the Hindu religious tradition and then to estimate him from the standpoint of later historical developments in the Indian sub-continent.

The modern period has seen quite a number of vigorous Hindu reform movements, from the Brahmo Samaj of Ram Mohan Roy to the metaphysical teachings and *ashram* of Sri Aurobindo in Pondicherry and beyond. In the period up to the Second World War we must also add Gandhi, even if he did not see himself primarily as a religious teacher. These movements were major ways in which Hinduism coped with the vicissitudes brought upon it by British rule and Western ideas and religious criticisms. They tended to reach back into various parts of India's past to bring forward an element that could be built upon in modern conditions. For Sarasvati Dayananda it was above all the Veda, interpreted without reference to the varied developments – such as temple worship and the cult of images – which arose during classical Hinduism but which were for Dayananda corruptions of the true faith. For Swami Vivekananda a paradigm was the teaching of Shankaracharya which, suitably adapted, became a remarkably subtle matrix for re-interpreting unity of all religions and the claim of Hinduism to be all-embracing and pluralistic. For Gandhi it was the ancient ideal of *ahimsa*, adapted to political conditions. But although Gandhi came to stress continence and a kind of asceticism, through his daily life and fasts, he did not adopt the traditional role of the *sadhu*.

The Acharya had some affinities with each of these figures but his style, thought and programmes were also very different. As far as religious conceptions and practices are concerned, his emphasis on *tapasya* was unique among the reformers. His feeling about it had ancient roots and was in the main stream of Hindu thinking on the subject; namely, that the exercise of self-control and mortification of the flesh brings actual, almost tangible power. Likewise for him sexual continence was a genuine source of energy and a kind

163

of spiritual magnetism. These are old themes but they were played down by many modern exponents of the Hindu tradition. Many such commentators, under the spell of Western religious idealism, paid more attention to the high, metaphysical doctrines of the faith, and the sense of spiritual power and energy was lost in the more rationalistic mood of neo-Hindu intellectuals, such as Radhakrishnan and even Vivekananda (whom Swami Pranavananda admired, as we have noted). So the Acharya's career, with its real struggles and heroic modes of self-discipline, was very different in spirit from that of the other major figures of the modern period. Moreover, the Acharya's emphasis on athletic ability side-by-side with spiritual discipline finds little echo elsewhere, save in the integral yoga of Aurobindo (but even here the primordial strength of the young Binode is far away from the Western-educated attitudes of Aurobindo). This desire to bring people, especially the young, into a rigorous and idealistic practice of ancient Indian spiritual and athletic – not to say martial – training was harnessed to a perception of needed political action.

So the first main comment about the Acharya is this – that he was the chief apostle of *tapasya* in the modern period, but he applied it in a positive, practical manner to contemporary problems. He had an advantage over Vivekananda and some other leaders. Vivekananda was very Western in his methods, and thus may have removed himself and the movement he founded too far from its Indian roots. The Acharya, by contrast, was always a thoroughly Hindu figure, one reason incidentally why his work is less well known in the West.

He was traditionally Hindu in thinking of the transmission of power and energy in a sacramental manner. On the whole, modern commentators on Hinduism have underplayed its strong sense of ritual. This is partly because in the West there has been a progressive watering-down of ritual practice and a distrust often of anything that can be seen to be 'ritualism'. The Acharya applied the principles of ritual to his own organisation and his own sense of destiny. Since he felt

164

himself to be chosen as an instrument of the Divine Will, and a channel of the energy of the All-Dispenser, he provided means for transmitting that power so that he could energise his followers and, more broadly, the Hindu nation. This was the primary meaning of his allowing himself to be worshipped as a god and given the frequent homage of his monks. In this way he became the sacramental head of the Sangha, which functioned like an extension of his own being. This kind of religious expression is unusual from a Western perspective but made sense from the viewpoint of the Acharya, since he thought that what Hindus needed above all was power and energy, not another set of ideas of which plenty were available already. So the second main comment about him is that he drew upon and transformed an ancient Hindu recognition of the power-transmitting character of sacramental ritual. Scarcely any other major leader in modern times has followed this sacramental and devotional path.

He drew on one or two Buddhist themes. His pragmatic insistence on tact in dealing with varying people and situations, as in his campaign against exploitation in the Hindu holy places, and the inspiration to found a Sangha to project his ideals and inner experience came from his understanding of the Buddha's life. The content of his teaching was much more Hindu than Buddhist, and yet the sense of mission was drawn from Buddhism. No doubt Buddhist ideals also helped to form his egalitarian ideas about Hindu society and his detestation of untouchability. With the exception of Dr Ambedkar, who led his untouchable followers into Buddhism in order to gain a better deal in life for them, he was the only major modern leader to use Buddhist vocabulary so freely. This gave a more universal character to his interpretation of the glories of the Indian past.

His inner conviction of having received something like a divine Descent into his own person was not unprecedented and it is natural in the Hindu framework to see the conspicuously holy person as more than a symbol of the Divine. But this sense of indwelling divinity combined with the qualities described above that made him different in the gallery of modern Hindu reformers to create a religious movement that blended austerity, energy, sacramentalism and devotionalism. He became the focus of much piety and devotion, especially among his immediate disciples and the rural crowds of Bengal.

His ideal of the *Dharma Rashtra* marks him out from most of the leaders of his time (though militant groups such as the Hindu Mahasabha also worked, but in a more extreme fashion, for a Hindu-dominated State). His nationalism was traditionalist in certain respects, looking back to a golden age of Hindu glory. But it also incorporated two ideas which need discussing. One was the open-endedness of the ideal State. To some extent he looked back to Ashoka for inspiration. While Ashoka was a Buddhist emperor he preached respect for all religious groups. Could there then be a Hindu analogue – a Hindu State which nevertheless ascribed dignity to the other traditions? This was the idea as expressed in the policies of the Sangha. Because of the Acharya's controversial recruitment of a defence corps he was eager not to be seen as aggressive towards or intolerant of Muslims. As we have seen, he often helped Muslims in his energetic relief work, especially in the early days. He was also fierce in his condemnation of oppression of the untouchables, another main case of communalism, the ugly face of piety and traditionalism. He espoused the doctrine that peace had to come between equals. In East Bengal this meant a better position for the Hindus, who were in the minority, with Jinnah's Muslim League showing its muscle. The Acharya's view was that just as Muslims and Christians were relatively well organised, so Hindus ought to be. Then a kind of coalition would be feasible. As it was he saw the Hindus as riven by dissension and class and caste divisions. So it was important for both humanitarian and national reasons to overcome these divisions in a spirit of equality.

How are we to estimate his judgement on this latter, rather controversial approach to community politics? Our picture of India has of course been dominated by Gandhi's presence.

We tend to see modern Indian politics through the lens of his non-violence and tactics of non-co-operation. But the events of independence and after, as he began clearly to recognise in those fateful and tragic months between the foundation of the Republic and the assassination, moved in a most un-Gandhian direction. What were founded in India were two States: the one, Pakistan, on an overtly Muslim basis – and later it was to carry this to a logical conclusion in the formation of an Islamic constitution under Zia – and the other, India, which was pluralistic yet necessarily dominated by Hindu culture and ideals. That State soon found itself at war over Kashmir, and increasingly moved away from the ideals of non-violence as understood by Gandhi. This is not to say that India became aggressive, although it did help to detach Bangladesh from Pakistan. But it showed that India accepted too the logic of power. It became a mixed Hindu and democratic State, and it has shown signs, because of its regional and fissiparous impulses, of needing a strong centre. That was supplied by Mrs Gandhi, until her assassination, and by her son Rajiv, both also, as it happens, helping to incarnate a dynastic succession in the Nehru family which seems like an analogue to the old, kingly system. Thus for practical purposes India seems to be acquiring at least the formal properties of a *Dharma Rashtra*, even if in some ways it may lack the substance. But if we count the plural philosophy of neo-Vedanta as expounded by Swami Vivekananda as the new substance of Hindu doctrines, then it may be that even the substance of a newly-interpreted *Dharma* may be getting woven into the fabric of India long after Gandhi. In this respect it could be argued that Swami Pranavananda was more prophetic of the shape of things to come than was the Mahatma.

Can we, then, see signs that the ideal order towards which he strove and which he helped to sum up and symbolise in his own crowned figure and royal robe may be developing as India goes beyond its Congress heritage? Will there be a more conscious attempt to realise the *Dharma* State, modified for operation in the changing modern world? Was

167

the Acharya in that sense the Prophet of a new age in Hindu evolution? As Aurobindo wrote:

'In the end nature (in a liberated soul) acts in perfect truth and its spontaneous freedom; for it obeys only the luminous power of the Eternal. The individual has nothing further to gain, no desire to fulfil; he has become a portion of the Impersonality or the Universal Personality of the Eternal. No other object but the manifestation and play of the Divine Spirit . . . can move him to action.'[7]

The consciousness which the Acharya wished to instil in the masses, the consciousness of being Hindus first and foremost, hopefully treating one another with equal dignity, was important in the development of modern religious thinking in India. He was not the first to think in this way, of course: but he boldly accepted that Hinduism is a definable entity, and that being a Hindu is definable, through consciousness of belonging to a particular and well-shaped tradition. Again, despite regionalism there is no doubt that this sense of 'Hinduness' is increasingly important to contemporary Indian followers of that tradition. He also saw that once we tread this path of accepting Hinduism as a single religion rather than a negative label for those who happen not to be Christians, Muslims and so on, then the move towards social justice and equality becomes crucial. Hindus could not afford to alienate untouchables by driving them to define themselves separately from the caste Hindus. Hinduism must, to gain true unity, reform itself in favour of the poor and the oppressed. To this ideal the Acharya gave expression through the establishment of the Hindu-Milan-Mandirs. He recognised that concrete institutional action was a precondition of giving the different classes a sense of brotherly and sisterly unity under the one banner of Hinduism. As other religious traditions were becoming increasingly well organised and articulated, through modern methods and in response to recent pressures, so also should Hinduism. It is a natural development but one that needs energising; and it was to this that the Acharya bent his efforts.

Because of his emphasis on the Hindu national ideal he was necessarily drawn to emphasising the vitality of the ancient heritage. A group gains its sense of identity through recalling, pondering and celebrating its past. Consciousness is thus shaped by sacred and historical narrative. To point to the Hindu past was therefore a necessary part of the preaching of the Sangha. Because it was for obvious reasons looking backwards, to the Veda, the Epics and so on, it could be criticised by enemies as 'reactionary'. Certainly the Acharya was not enamoured of the shape of modern education and the concepts of progress as understood in his time. In that respect he was not progressive, as commonly understood. But he was trying to resolve the problem of the regeneration of India now under foreign rule. He was not content just to take the ideas and the weapons of the foreigner and adopt them as Indian or Hindu. To do that would have been to sacrifice the tradition in the attempt to save it. On the other hand his reforming attitudes were themselves, in their own way, modernising: to build pilgrim rest houses in the holy places was to bring something new to the scene; his flood and famine relief work and his work among the poor pointed towards more systematic efforts to resolve age-old problems with up-to-date activities and institutions; his concern for breaking down caste barriers could also be regarded as modern in spirit. It was all done with a view to restoring a sense of pride; and that pride depended both on action today and on a recollection of ancient glories. In that sense he was a traditionalist. But he was a traditionalist with untraditional energy.

His ideals were of course implanted in the Sangha and another feature of his work is the drive to spread a sense of Hindu destiny overseas, in the founding of schools, such as the Hindu College in Guyana founded by Swami Purnananda, cultural centres and missions abroad, in such countries as Indonesia and the United Kingdom. The most important disciple in this work was Swami Advaitananda who, under the auspices of the Indian Cultural Mission, toured – East Africa, the East Indies (Indonesia), Fiji, the Andaman Islands, West Indies and Canada – where he opened branches. There is no doubt that both now and in the future the Hindu diaspora – Indians residing overseas, often in large numbers – plays and will play an increasingly important part in the global cultural and religious life of Hinduism.

Finally, it must be emphasized that the Acharya was one of the foremost figures in Hindu history who thought of service as being of the essence of the *Dharma*. This sense of service was particularly vital in his day, since Western attitudes to Hinduism tended towards the inappropriate judgement that it is a religion which turns away from the world. It is a cliché, but a false cliché, that Hinduism is world-negating. The Sangha belied this judgement in a double way. On the one hand it incarnated the *Dharma Rashtra* ideal, which is the reverse of world-negating; on the other, it linked the most profound austerity and the most absorbed sense of the Transcendent through meditation and prayer to the most energetic kind of social and medical service to others. There are of course other-worldly strands in the Hindu as in other religious traditions: but the Acharya stood for that more widespread sense in Hinduism that the *Dharma* runs like an electric pulse through the whole of cosmic and social existence.

The reflections just now expressed should not make us forget that young figure who had a mysterious vocation to train himself in the most formidable austerities by the swampy jungle that flanked an old Durga shrine near the heart of a straddling, green-girt village in a far part of East Bengal. That young person stood for many strange powers which can burst out of the Hindu way, which is quiet, primordial, incarnated in villages, shrouded in the early morning mists and the reddish dust of evening, so ancient, so variegated, a multi-coloured matrix of worldly and heavenly values. In the green Bengal countryside and by the Padma and its tributaries there grew in him the old ideals of *tapas*, devotion, service, divine power. And somewhere, floating as it were in the shafts of sunlight that came through the trees

170

and beside the thatched cottages, were the echoes and bright shadows of ancient kings and sonorous seers, and the voices of Vishnu and the Buddha, and the sound perhaps of the footsteps of that beast upon which the Goddess rode.

1   Swami Vedananda, 3rd edition (Bengali), p. 467.
2   ibid., p. 469.
3   ibid., p. 475.
4   ibid., p. 453.
5   Swami Nirmalanda, 1st edition, p. 295.
6   Swami Vedananda, pp. 282–3.
7   Aurobindo, The Synthesis of Yoga. (Pondicherry: 1948), p. 198.

BIBLIOGRAPHY

Danielou, Alain, *Hindu Polytheism* (London: Routledge and Kegan Paul, 1964).

Smart, Ninian, *The Religious Experience of Mankind*, 3rd edn. (New York: Charles Scribner's Sons, 1983).

Walker, Benjamin, *Hindu World* (2 vols) (London: George Allen & Unwin, 1968).

Swami Vikashananda, *Foundation of Religion* (Calcutta: Bharat Sevashram Sangha, 1979).

Swami Pranavananda, *The Sangha-Geeta* (Calcutta: Bharat Sevashram Sangha, 1967).

Swami Vedananda, *The Prophet of the Age* (Calcutta: Bharat Sevashram Sangha, n.d.).

Swami Nirmalananda, *Kanthe Kanthe Karuna Katha*.

Swami Advaitananda, *Sri Sri Pranavananda Lila Smriti* (these two Bengali works cited in the MS of Swami Purnananda).

Swami Purnananda, Unpublished Diary and Other Writings.